Romanian Armored Forces
In World War II

Dedicated to:
Solete (my life)
My parents Salud y Eduardo.
Merce, Caco y Ricardo.
June (munduko printzesa polita), Iñigo e Ibón

For his invaluable help in bringing this work to fruition: Marisol García Gómez, Ricardo Ramallo Gil, Dragos Pusca and Victor Nitu great experts in the Romanian army during WW2 (from worldwar2.ro), Mircea87 for his generosity in allowing the use of his photographs on Wikipedia, tankarchives, George for his generosity in allowing the use of his photographs (from historice.ro), MMN, José Antonio García Gálvez "Teto", Giuseppe Guiduccio and Andrés Jiménez Llorens (for their great work despite the difficulties), José Antonio Muñoz Molero, Kamil Stopiński, Maciej Łacina and Nicole Mucha.

EDUARDO M. GIL MARTÍNEZ

Romanian Armored Forces In World War II

FIRST EDITION
© by KAGERO Publishing, 2018

AUTHOR
Eduardo M. Gil Martínez

EDITORS
Eduardo M. Gil Martínez

TRANSLATION/PROOFREADING
Ricardo Ramallo Gil

COVER
Łukasz Maj

DTP
Kagero Studio

COLOR PROFILES
Color profiles: Arkadiusz Wróbel

PHOTO SOURCE
Public domain; Courtesy by Pusca and Nitu from worldwar2.ro; Bundesarchiv; Courtesy by
George from Historice.ro; Courtesy of tankarchives

ISBN 978-83-951575-3-0

DISTRIBUTION
Kagero Publishing
ul. Akacjowa 100, os. Borek, Turka, 20-258 Lublin 62, Poland
phone +48 601-602-056, phone/fax +48 81 501-21-05
e-mail: marketing@kagero.pl
www.kagero.pl

Contents

ANNEXES

Preface

The performance of the German armored forces during World War II(WWII) is well known. What has not yet been so widespread is the behavior of the armored forces of Germany´s allied countries. While it is true that the performance of these was usually quite secondary when not disappointing, we should highlight the behavior of the Romanian armored forces. In recent times, authors such as Mark Axworthy, Mihai T. Filipescu or Patrick Cloutier, have deepened in this aspect, bringing light to a subject quite unknown even to fans of the history of World War II and the Axis in particular. We must also recognize the important work that Dragos Pusca and Victor Nitu have done and carry out in their website worldwar2. ro, which has managed to fill in many of the voids of the history of the armored forces and in general of the Romanian Armed Forces during the World War II. We want to compile in a didactic way but without academic intention, the information that in the previous works and in other diverse sources have been emerging about the Romanian Armored Forces, trying to focus on their diverse actions during the world conflict both in the Axis and together with the USSR.

The reluctance of the Germans to allow the arrival of their most modern and powerful weapons to any other country is well known; fact that motivated that the very worn Romanian armored units lacked an adequate combat abilities until 1944 when the Romanian armored arsenal finally benefited from the acquisition of tanks and tank destroyers from Germany. But, as we will read, it was too late.

While it is true that the present text will deal with Romanian armored forces, it is necessary on many occasions to deal with other Soviet and German military groups in order to provide a more general view of the fighting than we would have if we only circumscribed ourselves to them.

In this text, we will rescue the Romanian participation from oblivion during the World War II; from the beginning of the invasion of the USSR participating in the conquest of the vast Soviet lands, to the disbandment of the Axis in Ukraine two years after, seeking shelter in their own national territory. In these combats, the Romanian 1st Armored Division (the main Romanian armored unit during the World War II) on more than one occasion was practically destroyed with the need to be rebuilt on several occasions too. And as the swan song of the Romanian armored forces, the bloody battles against their former German and Hungarian allies after the defection of Romania, which would almost lead to the annihilation of the Romanian armor. The fight in many times of obsolete tanks against the T-34 or even Soviet IS-2, was evidently lost from the beginning but it did not mean that the Romanian tankers gave the best of them. We can appreciate how the Romanian tanks were used in many cases to help the infantry more than as it happened in the German Panzer units that acted together creating a Schwerpunkt (a point where the maximum effort of the armored unit was concentrated, with all the tanks concentrated and never allowing them to disperse despite the enemy's attack), motivated by obsolete doctrines after the development of the German Blitzkrieg that were destined to fail.

After Romania switched side in 1944, Romanian troops among which were some armored units were also forced to fight until the end of the war with the Soviets although virtually without any possibility of repair or reinforcement in their armored vehicles. These last actions of combat of the Romanian tanks would lead to the practical annihilation of the Romanian armored forces.

We will also remember the incipient Romanian military industry that despite not having the capacity to manufacture national tanks and armored vehicles as, for example, its Hungarian neighbor did, managed to create several self-propelled guns from captured Soviet military material. Even one of these, the Mareşal reached such high performance, that even Germany was interested in acquiring copies of this tank destroyer.

Despite being undervalued in many cases, Romanian soldiers fought at a good level within their means. In all situations in which the Romanians had to fight and engage in battles very often under difficult conditions, they did so with great courage despite the enemy's superiority in men and in modern armament. It is true that since the end of 1943 and especially until half of 1944 there was a political-military movement in Romania that was trying to abandon the Axis. This fact was the cause in many cases that some Romanian troops did not want to oppose a great resistance to the Soviet offensive in August 1944 or some others withdrew without wanting to fight. In the case of the Romanian armored forces, such a situation never occurred, trying to offer the greatest resistance to the Soviet advance and even carrying out counterattacks destined to failure but allowing the retreat to their comrades. Serve this text as a tribute and as a reminder of these men immersed in a confrontation whose consequences marked the future of the 45 subsequent years of the country's history.

CHAPTER I

The Birth Of The Romanian Armored Forces

Using as sources for the text the works of Nitu, Pusca, Axworthy, Cloutier, Zaloga and Filipescu, and adding information from other several sources, we know that the history of the Romanian armored forces during World War II (WWII) was marked by the secondary role to which Germany relegated its European allies. Advances in military technology during the years of the conflict were so rapid that the industry of countries such as Hungary, Romania or Italy, could not at any time be at the level of development or of course the amount of production reached by the Soviet or American. This caused a great dependence on the German industry to support them, but the circumstances of the war prevented this support was sufficient for these satellite countries could be equated with his Soviet rival.

The World War I (WWI) left in many countries new concepts in the form of combat, one of them being the use of tank. The Romanian military, like those of other countries that had lived close to the WWI did not doubt that definitely and above other weapons, the tank was the weapon of the future; especially after being able to appreciate its importance at the time of "breaking" with the trench warfare in which the world conflict had become. Romania participated in the WWI on the side of the Allies and had a heterogeneous armored arsenal of 34 armored vehicles (not tanks) of mainly Soviet origin. To be more precise, Romania remained neutral until 1916, when it joined the Allies under the promise of territorial gains (cited in the secret Treaty of Bucharest). In its intervention in the WWI after some initial military successes, the Romanian Army was repelled by the troops of the Central Powers, managing to lose up to two thirds of its territory (although in 1917 and with the help of the Russian forces, they already managed to take the initiative again after the battles of Mărăşti and Mărăşeşti).

After the WWI and following the agreement in the Treaty of Saint Germain of 1919, the winners guaranteed the adhesion of the territories previously promised to Romania (where the Austrian Bukovina or Bucovina in Romanian language was included). But these territories that passed under the Romanian dominion were increased after the Treaty of Trianon of 1920, with Transilvania and Banato (previously under Hungarian dominion). They would also receive the Bessarabia region from Russia (in this case by the Treaty of Paris). After all these territorial incorporations, Romania reached its greatest geographical extension period. These new lands incorporated to their nation motivated a period of greater wealth that allowed them to carry out important reforms in different areas in which of course was the military. After the WWI and the setbacks suffered in it, it was considered necessary to have a professional and modern army, equipped with the best possible means.

With respect to the germ of Romanian armored forces after the world conflict, the 34 artisanal armored vehicles that they owned were in a bad shape, notwithstanding this, in 1919 they were framed in two armored companies. Despite this first attempt to organize their armored vehicles, the result was not very prominent, so their effectiveness in combat was practically nil due to the factors mentioned above such as the heterogeneous and stripped of the vehicles. Faced with this situation, the Romanian Government decided that it was necessary to boost its incipient branch of the Army for what in the spring of 1919 decided to provide the Romanian Army with an armored branch that should be equipped mainly with tanks.

Since a new project was started, starting almost from nothing, the military specialists in charge of bringing this development of the armored weapon to a successful conclusion set their sights on the French ally. France was pleased to see this offer for which it would lend its support for the creation of a Romanian Tank School. In concrete the name that received this School was the "School of assault vehicles" ("Scoli of Care of asalt") and would have its base in the locality of Giorgiu. This one began to operate on July 21, 1919, training new officers in the use of tanks. Only a week later, on August 1, 1919, a "Battalion of combat vehicles" (batalionul de care de lupta) was created, which would be the 1st Tank Regiment or Regiment 1 Care of Lupta in the Romanian language (but this attempt enhance the armored weapon will not be as fast as they pretended since the 2nd Tank Regiment would be created as early as November 1939).

Being the Romanian Government decided to progress in the field of battle tanks, it acquired 74-76 FT-17 light tanks from France (out of them 45 or 48 according to other sources were endowed with the Puteaux 37 mm gun, while the others were only armed with 8mm Hotchkiss machine guns). Seventeen of these battle tanks were rebuilt and tuned in the recently created Leonida Workshops (Ateliere Leonida) and in the Army State Arsenal, located in Bucharest. It was with these armored vehicles, with which the 1st Regiment of tanks was established on August 1, 1919. These tanks would immediately join the "Battalion of combat vehicles", which was divided into 4 companies. As a curiosity comment the Battalion was initially framed within the Artillery weapon, to pass in 1922 to belong to the Infantry (this fact marked in many aspects the future use that the Romanians would make of their battle tanks as we will see later). The FT-17 served to "initiate" the Romanians in the actual handling of the tanks and to such an extent came this training, which in 1925 was already considered very battered, so that only 34 active tanks and vehicles remained in active service in 1930. Again Romania was at a minimum level of armored equipment, while the political events in Europe began to generate a large arms escalation that would lead to the World War II (WWII). So at the beginning of the decade of the 30s we found the Romanian Army that was still based more on its human potential than on the modernity of its materials; thus this one was equipped with multiple weapons of diverse origins and calibers, which logistically did not favor them at all. This fact motivated, as on the other hand it is reasonable, that some units were much better equipped than others. In spite of it and of general way the army continued leaning mainly on the horses (horse towed weapons) being very few the units that counted on some type of motorized vehicle. This fact that at the beginning of the 30s was already very disturbing, was not solved properly, so that in the WWII the Romanian troops had to count on horses again as the "engine" of most of their troops.

An important aspect when machining an army is not only to have the vehicles, but also to have facilities to manufacture them, repair them and obtain spare parts for them. In spite of the impulse that the acquisition of the new territories supposed, Rumania still continued being a country eminently based on agriculture where these industries only existed in a way so incipient that it incapacitated them for any attempt of national production of some armored vehicle. Here, the aforementioned Leonida Workshops played an important role, which in many cases worked in an artisanal way. We will cite as curiosity the only thing that could look like an industry at that time, which was the Ford plant that was in Romania for the construction of vehicles from imported components.

As early as 1934, despite attempts to boost the national industry forward, Romanian experts in the field confirmed the inability for the national production of armored vehicles, making acquisition abroad necessary and urgent given the events that were occurring in the other European countries of the environment.

Meanwhile, the few tanks that still had Romania were increasingly less operational time due to its intense use. All the good intentions of the Romanian Government were going to be ruined, and to top it off and without noticing it another problem was "accommodating" between the Romanian armored forces, which would only take a few years to face. We refer to the military doctrine that would guide the operational use of the armored forces that was based on the acquired learning of their French friends; in which the infantry had predominance over any other military branch, so the tanks were only a support for them and they would not have independent operative capacity (fact that after the masterful use that the Germans gave of their armor at the beginning of WWII, was immediately out of phase). So that from the knowledge acquired in these years, the future Romanian armor would be used as support for the infantry and usually divided into small units under the control of infantry or artillery forces (which resulted in the non-existence of specific tactics for the armored units). As we will write throughout the text, this fact will pass a terrible bill during the years of the WWII.

After reconsidering what was necessary to increase its armored force, it would be in 1935 when an ambitious 10-year army rearmament program was approved. The purpose of the program would be to rearm with modern and homogeneous material to the army, get an adequate motorization and mechanization in the in-fantry and artillery units and of course the improvement of the Romanian armored units. This program was planned to be carried out with part of the profits obtained from the sale of oil from the Ploieşti fields and, a priori, it was not unreasonable, provided that everything followed its correct course, which would be verified every year. As we have said, the Romanian industrial capacity was minimal, which meant that material purchases should be made abroad in almost all cases (for example, the national manufacture of trucks before the war was limited to a single factory with very limited production). During those pre-WWII years, Czechoslovakia had become a major manufacturer and exporter of weapons of all kinds (airplanes, battle tanks, small arms, etc.) so Romania acquired virtually all the material to carry out the start-up of the upgrade plan (either by direct importation or by manufacturing license). These agreements allowed them to train a large number of technicians and mechanics who managed to manufacture Romanian auto armored vehicles on chassis of foreign-made vehicles (such as TACAM vehicles).

Regarding the battle tanks, a hasty decision was not taken but instead a group of Romanian officers with knowledge of the armored weapon visited several European companies (Ursus, Vickers, Renault, ČKD and Škoda) to find the tank that best suits the needs of the country. As it happened in the "search" of other weapons, it was again Czechoslovakia that fulfilled better the expectations (both of quality level and good manufacturing, as well as in political aspects and of geographical proximity) of supplying an adequate battle tank for Romania. The ČKD and Škoda companies were the chosen ones after which they were sent a formal proposal on January 8, 1936 with the demands demanded by the Romanian Army. In less than five months (May 30, 1936) a vehicle from each company received Romanian approval; and on August 14, 1936 the agreements were signed in Prague for which the ČKD would supply 35-36 Prague AH-IV tanks (which in Romania would be called "fane de recunasfere R-1", although the company itself called them AH-IV-R) and the Škoda would provide 126 light tanks LT-35 ("fane usor R-2" for Romanians and Š-IIa-R for Czechoslovaks). The first, lightest vehicles would be destined to serve in the Cavalry, while the LT-35 would fulfill its tasks in the Tank Regiment.

Regarding the R-2, the Romanian Army insisted on making some modifications to the original model, which led to the fact that starting from vehicle number 64, the R-2 was renamed R-2c (cimentate). So the R-2c included those modifications among which was a different configuration of the turret, the redesign of the back of the turret with some other minor modifications.

Once the Romanian armor plan of modernization was initiated, it was not stopped after the first acquisitions because in 1938 not less than 200 Renault R-35 were requested to the old French friend. But before the fall of France to the hands of the German troops, only 41 could be supplied (50 according to some sources, although less probable). The luck that in this case did not favor Rumania, would do it in 1939 when they received 35 Polish R-35 who after fleeing their country by the German invasion ended up "captured" by the Rumanians when crossing the Rumanian border.

On the other hand, the production rights under license of the small Malaxa Type UE (Renault UE), which would perform the functions of transport, reconnaissance vehicle, artillery tractor, etc., were obtained. In order to be able to manufacture under license, a Company called Franco-Romana was created, which aimed to manufacture R-35 and Malaxa. Finally, 60 copies of Malaxa were obtained, but the manufacture in Romania of the R-35 never materialized.

With respect to trucks, Romania was in a situation similar to that of its armored vehicles, since before the war began it was in possession of some 3,000 trucks. The small number of motor vehicles will become a significant burden in the upcoming campaigns in which Romania took part in the USSR.

CHAPTER II

1938. Drums Of War In Europe

In 1938 a Romanian delegation traveled to Czechoslovakia with the intention of achieving production under license of the R-1 and R-2 models (already in service in the Romanian Army). The intention was to reach the number of 300 R-1 and 280 R-2. But the events in the convulsed Europe, with the crisis of the Sudetenland and the subsequent annexation of Bohemia and Moravia by the German Reich, stopped any Romanian attempt to achieve its objectives, due that the Czechoslovak war industry was under the direct control of the Reich.

A Renault FT-17 at the National Military Museum in Bucharest. These obsolete tanks were mainly used in internal security missions in industrial zones and urban centers in Romania as in Bucharest, Ploieşti, Sibiu or Reşiţa. [From public domain – by mircea87]

Photograph of Conducator Ion Antonescu posing with Romanian and German medals, which directed the fate of Romania during a great part of WW2. [From public domain (taken by Dr. Radu Mihai Crisan)]

Several Czechoslovak OA vz.30 armored vehicles, similar to those that Romania obtained after the flight of a Czech armored company in March 1939 that ended up seeking refuge in Romania. [From public domain]

Photograph showing several R-2 tanks on the assembly line of the Škoda R-2 Factory in February 1939. These tanks would be those that were sent to Romania and would form part of the Romanian 1st Armored Division. [From public domain]

Marshal Ion Antonescu, had an escort unit (called Batalionul de gardă al Mareşalului Antonescu or Regimentul de gardă al Conducătorului Statului) in which there were several second-class armored vehicles, as narrated in the text. [Courtesy by Pusca and Nitu from worldwar2.ro]

Map of Romania with territorial losses suffered in 1940 by Bulgarians, Hungarians and Soviets.

Parade of celebration of the signature by Romania of the Tripartite Pact, where Ion Antonescu fourth and the Romanian monarch, Miguel I fifth (fourth and fifth people from the left of the photo) are appreciated. [From public domain]

Photograph of the Romanian King Carol II who abdicated in favor of his son Mihail I on September 6, 1940. [From public domain]

ORDIN CĂTRE ARMATĂ

Ostași,
V'am făgăduit din prima zi a noii domnii și a luptei mele naționale, să vă duc la biruință.
Să șterg pata de desonoare din cartea Neamului și umbra de umilire de pe fruntea și epoleții voștri.
Azi a sosit ceasul celei mai sfinte lupte, lupta drepturilor strămoșești și a bisericii, lupta pentru vetrele și altarele românești de totdeauna.

Ostași,
Vă ordon:
Treceți Prutul,
Sdrobiți vrăjmașul din Răsărit și Miază-Noapte.
Desrobiți din jugul roșu al bolșevismului, pe frații noștri cotropiți.
Reîmpliniți în trupul țării glia străbună a Basarabilor și codrii Voevodali ai Bucovinei, ogoarele și plaiurile voastre.

Ostași,
Plecați azi pe drumul biruințelor lui Ștefan cel Mare, ca să cuprindeți cu jertfa voastră, ceeace au supus strămoșii noștri cu lupta lor.
Înainte!
Fiți mândri că veacurile ne-au lăsat aci straja dreptății și zid de cetate creștină.
Fiți vrednici de trecutul românesc.

Ostași,
Veți lupta cot la cot, suflet la suflet, lângă cea mai puternică și glorioasă armată a lumii.
Îndrăsniți să vă măsurați vitejia și să vă dovediți mândria, camarazilor voștri.
Ei luptă pe pământul moldovean, pentru granițele noastre și pentru dreptatea lumii.
Fiți vrednici de cinsta pe care v'au făcut-o istoria, armata Marelui Reich și neîntrecutul ei comandant Adolf Hitler.

Ostași,
Înainte!
Să luptați pentru gloria Neamului;
Să muriți pentru vatra părinților și a copiilor voștri;
Să cinstiți prin vitejia voastră, amintirea lui Mihai Vodă și a lui Ștefan cel Mare, a martirilor și eroilor căzuți în pământul veciniciei noastre, cu gândul țintă la Dumnezeu.
Să luptați pentru desrobirea fraților noștri, a Basarabiei și Bucovinei, pentru cinstirea bisericilor, a vieții și căminurilor batjocorite de păgânii cotropitori.
Să luptați pentru a ne răsbuna umilirea și nedreptatea.
V'o cere Neamul, Regele și Generalul vostru.

Ostași,
Isbânda va fi a noastră.
La luptă.
Cu Dumnezeu înainte!

General Ion Antonescu, 22 Iunie 1941.

Document where we can see the order of June 22, 1941 from General Ion Antonescu to the Romanian army to cross the river Prut and take Bessarabia. [From public domain]

Photograph where we see Romanian soldiers groups advancing. Although morale was high when they took Bessarabia, it began to diminish when they had to penetrate inside the USSR. [Bundesarchiv, N 1603 Bild-241 Horst Grund CC-BY-SA 3.0.]

Soviet parade with several tanks on the streets of Chisináu (Kishinev) in 1940. On July 16, 1941 the 1st Armored Division participated in the capture of the current capital of Moldova. [Courtesy by George from Historice.ro]

Romanian Cavalry Troops cross a bridge in the Eastern Front. The Romanian cavalry units had the support of the R-1 tanquettes for armed reconnaissance tasks. [Courtesy by George from Historice.ro]

The most powerful tank in the Romanian arsenal at the beginning of the war was the R-2. In this photograph we see a column of R-2s, which pass by a Skoda truck during its march near Chisinau (Kishinev), in Bessarabia in July 1941. We can see on the side of the tank in the foreground the silhouette of the Michael Cross, Badge of the Romanian troops. [Courtesy by George from Historice.ro]

A column of Romanian R-2 tanks marches down a street in Chisinau (Kishinev) in 1941. In the tank closest to the photographer you can see the Michael Cross painted on the engine compartment to facilitate aerial reconnaissance of Romanian tanks. [Courtesy by George from Historice.ro]

One of the many 76.2 mm guns captured by the Soviets and used by the Romanian Army; in this case during the crossing of Tisa river. Several of these guns ended up in the TACAM tank hunters T-60 and TACAM R-2. [Courtesy by Pusca and Nitu from worldwar2.ro from MMN]

The vast Ukrainian lands allowed the obsolete Romanian mechanized force to suffer a multitude of breaks and breakdowns in the vehicles even before contacting the enemy. In the photo we see some soldiers in observation tasks of the enemy. [Courtesy by Pusca and Nitu from worldwar2.ro]

Well-known photograph where King Mihai I (Michael I) is seen standing next to General Ion Antonescu sitting watching Romanian troops in the front, July 1941. [Courtesy by Pusca and Nitu from worldwar2.ro From Signal magazine via Ion Fonosch]

A R-1 tank during the performance of an exercise where he demonstrated his good performance. These small armored vehicles were incorporated into the Cavalry Brigades reconnaissance squads. Its usefulness in tasks of reconnaissance in combat was well demonstrated, but its thin armoring turned out to be an important inconvenience. [Courtesy by Pusca and Nitu from worldwar2.ro from MMN]

Two R-35 tanks tow a captured Russian BT-2 tank. During the war Romania captured a high number of Soviet armored vehicles, but only part of them were put in service against their former owners. This photo was taken in Bessarabia, July 1941. [Courtesy by Pusca and Nitu from worldwar2.ro]

Romanian R-2 tank crew poses in front of their tank together with a German instructor during summer 1941. Before the combats for Stalingrad, the Romanian 1stArmored Division had 109 R-2s. [Courtesy by Pusca and Nitu from worldwar2.ro from Armata Romana 1941-1945]

The Romanian first blood in WW2 was spilled out in the clashes against the Soviets during the offensive for Bessarabia, July 1941. During the summer 1941, the R-2s supporting Romanian Infantry troops (like the shown in this picture) managed to destroy a lot of Soviets armored vehicles. [Courtesy by Pusca and Nitu from worldwar2.ro from MMN]

The Romanian cavalry units were not fully motorized so the horse was intensely used as a transport main. The R-1 tanquettes belonging to Cavalry units were used as reconnaissance vehicles. In the picture a column of cavalry troops cross a bridge heading to the Bessarabian front. [Courtesy by Pusca and Nitu from worldwar2.ro]

The R-35 tank, despite its low qualities for modern armored warfare, demonstrated in the combats by Odessa the importance of good armoring. This one was photographed by mircea at the King Ferdinand Museum. [From public domain – by mircea87]

Photograph of a T-60 in Kubinka. This armored vehicle from which Romania captured several, was completely obsolete for use in combat. Despite this, Romania built an acceptable tank destroyer, the TACAM T-60 from this tank. [From public domain – by Saiga20K]

Photograph of a STZ-5 armored tractor taken in Odessa in August 1941. Between 70 and 120 (according to Axworthy) STZ tractors were added a 37 mm cannon or machine guns.
[From public domain]

The Soviet tank T-38, from which the Romanians had captured some specimens. Despite having the same name, do not confuse it with the T-38 or Pz.kpfw.38 (t). [From public domain – by one half 3544]

A Soviet artillery gun belonging to the powerful defenses of Odessa with its crew of artillerymen in 1941. [From public domain]

CHAPTER III

1939. World War II Begins

On August 23, 1939 a secret pact of non-aggression was signed between the USSR and Germany (Ribbentrop-Molotov pact) in which both nations shared influences in Eastern Europe. On September 1 in the same year the German attack against Poland took place, which was the beginning of WWII. The Polish army was quickly defeated by the Germans, but they found out that the Soviet giant had also invaded them by their eastern region until they seized power in that area of the country. Before all these political and military movements the Romanian Government allowed civilians and Polish troops to use their territory to flee along with the country's gold reserves. Among the military units that fled from Poland fell into Romanian power, were the aforementioned 35 R-35 battle tanks of the 21st Armored Battalion of the Polish Army. With this unexpected addition, the number of R-35 Romanian tanks amounted to about 73 copies.

They also arrived fleeing from Poland some other armored vehicles, although of second level, consisting mainly in about 10-15 copies of the TK and TKS tanks.

The beginning of the WWII with the German Blitzkrieg showed how important the armored forces would be in the newly initiated conflict. The Romanian government took note of this and as a first step a "Tank Training Center" was created in the vicinity of the town of Târgoviste, where special emphasis could be placed on the new armored techniques that the Germans had in use. After that, the next thing was to restructure its armored forces, which would be grouped at the end of 1939 in a large Brigade called 1st Motorized Brigade (Brigade 1 motomecanizata), which included the 1st Tank Regiment equipped with 126 R-2 (Škoda LT VZ 35) and the 2nd Tank Regiment (created on November 1, 1939) endowed with 75 R-35 (including both those purchased from France as well as the "gifts" from Poland). On the other hand, the venerable FT 17 were assigned to a training unit called the FT tank battalion (Batalionul Carelor de Lupta FT), reaching a theoretical number of 75 but a real number of about 20-30 in service, which would fulfill the functions of security in the interior of the country (in 1944 these armored relics still fulfilled surveillance tasks in the Romanian capital).

Although this restructuring at first glance may seem very appropriate, it really was not so much since these tanks were not acting as independent units but were divided between different infantry units (the crews of the tanks only received training to support to the infantry, following the outdated ideas that were acquired years ago copying the French).

Both the R-2 and the R-35 were equipped with 37 mm guns, but to be honest, only the guns of the R-2 had some antitank capability, the rest being more suitable for use as support guns to the infantry (exactly what the Romanians wanted according to their military doctrine). Also the R-2 exceeded the R-35 in speed and better radio equipment, both elements very necessary if they wanted in some way to emulate the concept of the Blitzkrieg.

CHAPTER IV

1940. Romania Falls Under The German Influence

After the fall of France in June 1940 and the subsequent withdrawal of British troops in the continent, Romania was left without its most important allies, within the convulsed Europe. When losing the protection especially of France, the new "owners" of the continent began to move their pieces. The USSR occupied Bessarabia (Basarabia in Romanian) and northern Bukovina on June 28, while on August 30 it was Hungary that took northern Transylvania, and on September 7, Bulgaria took over southern Dobruja. In just three months Romania had lost without being able to do anything against, a third of the size of its country, and what was worse, the Country was alone in a Europe at war.

The political instability that was brewing in the interior of Romania between the nationalist Iron Guard and King Carol II, led the latter to feel very pressured to abandon power and abdicate. So on September 6, 1940, King Carol II abdicated in favor of his son Mihail I. That same day, General and Prime Minister Ion Antonescu received unlimited powers acting from that moment as regent in the country. Antonescu formed a new government in which included representatives of the Iron Guard or also called "Legion of the Archangel Michael" (nationalist group close to German ideas). After the visit on October 12 of a German military and diplomatic delegation, on November 23, 1940, beset by the situation of the country in Europe and internal political changes, it adhered to the so-called Tripartite Pact. By then, the German military was already training the Romanian troops, as well as protecting the Romanian oil fields (which seemed necessary for the functioning of the German machine, and which Hitler was willing to control directly).

The German delegation that arrived in October, was in charge of initiating the Romanians in the arts of the Blitzkrieg, as well as in changing the previous ideas of the use of the armored forces for more new ones in which the support to the infantry went to a second place. Evidently this fact was a breath of fresh air in the stagnant mentality of the Romanian Army, but neither would arrive at the desired end for a main reason: the Romanians thought that after the learning the Germans would provide German tanks, which did not happen immediately. In addition, the Germans did not manage to undo the imbricated union that Romanian tanks and infantry had, so the basic problem still existed. Due to these reasons, friction between Romanians and Germans began to appear, although the latter also did not care much to bother a country that had become a German satellite. In spite of it, the Romanian training led by the Germans continued until May of 1941.

It is important to remember that Romania had been Germany's enemy during the WWI and that in the years before the WWII had signed a mutual defense treaty with other countries such as Czechoslovakia, Greece, Turkey, Yugoslavia and Poland in the face of a possible aggression by Germany, Hungary, the USSR or Bulgaria. From one day to the next, many of the natural enemies of Romania (the conflict with Hungary over Transylvania kept both countries very close to the armed confrontation despite belonging to the Axis) had become "faithful" allies; a fact that many Romanian military failed to fully assimilate.

Returning to the armored forces, during the year 1940 more R-35s were received by the Romanian Army, which allowed the 2nd Tank Regiment to gradually grow.

CHAPTER V

1941. Birth And Attrition

Birth Of The Armored Division

The WWII continued and Romania was still out of the conflict. But the increase in hostilities made the Romanian military high command realize that a remodeling of their armored forces was necessary, so that on April 17, 1941 the 1st Armored Division or Divizia 1 blindata (from the Motor-Mechanized Brigade whose denomination was changed) was officially created. This was constituted by the 1st and 2nd Tank Regiments, in addition of the Vanatori 3rd and 4th Motorized Regiments. Complementing these main units were the 1st Motorized Artillery Regiment, the Special Weapons Battalion, the Motorized Reconnaissance Group, the Communications Company, the Service Group, the Traffic Squad, the Police Squad, the Detachment of fuel and other repair work, the Food Supply Group, the Ammunition Supply Group, the Ambulance Section, the Auto Section, the Truck Company and the Motorized Engineers Battalion. On paper, the Division seemed an important armored force, but it was deficient in many aspects, especially in combat and support vehicles; so that although called Division, for the Germans it was a reinforced Regiment, while the Soviets would consider it as a Brigade. Other elements that weighed against the Division were its poor radio communications (for which there was no previous training to the crews), the hypomobile dependence it suffered or the shortage of supplies. The cooperation between the infantry and the battle tanks was never good, being slightly practical when this was done in the with infantry platoons; but without the Armored Division fully engaged in even any type of training. Despite all these elements that were not good for the Romanians, the morale among the troops was quite good. In total the Division had 283 officers, 433 non-commissioned officers, 6,014 soldiers, 5,367 rifles, 234 light machine guns, 39 heavy machine guns, 18 mortars, 36 artillery pieces, tanks (only 109 R-2 operational by early June 1941) and others 725 vehicles of various types. The Division was under the command of Brigadier General Ioan Sion (who would remain in office until January 10, 1942).

In order to try to use the different armored vehicles as good as possible, the R-1 tanks were sent to the Cavalry reconnaissance units, where they were completely dispersed without the possibility of acting together. This is the reason why during the text we will not treat them specifically.

In order to "rise" the Division, the Romanians received aid from the 64th Panzer Grenadier Regiment, the 4th Panzer Regiment and the 4th German Antiaircraft Artillery Regiment.

Following the works of Nitu, Pusca, Axworthy, Cloutier, Zaloga and Filipescu we know that due to the great operational difference between the two main types of tanks used by the Romanians (the R-2 and the R-35), it was decided to leave the R-35 (and therefore the 2nd Tank Regiment) assigned to the 4th Army in tasks purely in support of the infantry who would participate in the coming combats for Southern Bessarabia and Odessa. For its part, the 1st Tank Regiment was inside the 1st Armored Division, becoming its only element constituted by battle tanks (this fact was the reason why during the 1941campaigns, the 1st Armored Division would only use the R-2).

Each Regiment was constituted by two Tank Battalions, and each Battalion was constituted by three Car Companies and one Maintenance Company. But also in it there were differences between the 1st and 2nd Regiment. The 1st Tank Regiment had five platoons per Company (with three tanks each), while the 2nd Tank Regiment only had three platoons per Company.

In support of the battle tanks, each Tank Regiment also had four Schneider anti-tank 47 mm pieces model 1936 and 2 Hotchkiss 13.2 mm anti-aircraft machine guns model 1939. Talking about the Battalion, they were also equipped with four antiaircraft machine guns.

Before the critical situation that was approaching with the entrance in the war of Rumania, they tried to acquire 216 tanks T-21 (for which already the Romanians had already shown interest), as well as 395 light tanks LT vz 38 (also denominated Panzer kpfw.38(t) or Pz.kpfw.38(t) by the Germans). These models would have represented a considerable improvement of the armored potential of Romania, but again the Germans put all kinds of obstacles that together with the beginning of the German offensive against the USSR, prevented the Romanians from achieving their wishes.

First Combat Actions

The drums of war began to sound on the Eastern Front and troop movements were evident. In the spring of 1941 about 370000 German soldiers were stationed in Romania. Despite the Romanian 1st Armored Division did not take part in the operation "Barbarrossa" which started on June 22, 1941 by which it proceeded to the invasion of the USSR; although in a few days it would take part in the struggle against the Soviets (an attitude similar to the one of his Hungarian "allies", who declared war on the USSR on June 27).

A very important fact to keep in mind is that the ancestral rivalry between both countries was intact despite being fighting in the USSR on the same side and even shoulder to shoulder troops of both armies in some cases. The hatred was mutual and even the main idea of the Hungarian Regent Horthy in the middle of the war against the USSR was based on the fact that the best Hungarian units should be in national territory to prevent any kind of attack from Romania.

During the campaign of 1941 the 1st Armored Division was used following the German military doctrine, that is, as a unit of shock against the enemy. This use obtained significant successes in the context of the battles for the conquest of Bessarabia (framed in the operation "Munich" for the capture of Bessarabia and Northern Bukovina, which took place after the "tranquility" in the months of June and July when the front remained relatively static) and later in the siege of Odessa between July and October 1941. The 1st Armored Division took part in the military operations carried out by Romania from the beginning of its intervention in the attack on the USSR, within the mixed German-Romanian formation constituted by the German XI Army and the 3rd and 4th Romanian Armies. On July 3 the Romanian Army crossed the Prut River and began an advance towards Mogilev Podolski on Ukrainian lands. The 1st Armored Division crossed the Prut the same day and advanced towards Bratuseni-Edinita and did not have to wait long for the first Romanian tank battle against the Soviet tanks, which took place between 4 and July 5 in the vicinity of the town of Brynzjena where a platoon of R-2 was confronted against 12 Soviet tanks that supported troops of the 74th and 176th Rifle Divisions (belonging to the 48th Rifle Corps). The result was the loss of an R-2 in exchange for the destruction of two T-28.

Continuing its advance, positions were taken in the towns of Chetrosita Veche and Parcova, reaching its vanguard at the town of Edinita. The next day, the Dnestr River had been hit, as had its German allies. On July 7, the 1st Romanian Armored Division was positioned in the pre-1940 borders in the vicinity of Mogilev.

The Romanian 1st Armored Division was then ordered to move southwards towards Mosana-Soroca (Soroki). From there on July 10, they managed to block retreating Soviet troops (from the 176th Rifle Division) heading towards Mogilev while clearing the right side of the Dnestr River in the Soroca area (Soroki). After that, they were subordinated to the 54th German Corps, with which on July 12 they participated in the capture of the town of Balti (Beltsy), to continue their harassment of the Soviets deployed in the town of Calarasi on July 14 where they lost 2 R-2 due to the Soviet artillery fire.

In all these combats, the tanks were highlighted in small operative groups, which along with the deplorable lack of collaboration between tanks and the infantry, caused very severe casualties in both men and material in the brand new 1st Armored Division. In addition, the R-35 was evident (despite its powerful armor), due to its low speed that in some cases prevented them from taking part in mobile operations, but even following the velocity of the infantry. This motivated that definitively the R-35 happened to second place after the R-2.

The progress of the Romanians through Ukraine proceeded favorably until various Soviet counterattacks in the Dnestr River area caused this progress to come to a complete standstill. After that, the 1st Armored Division was forced to change its initial direction, looking for operational zones with less difficult objectives, such as the capture of Chisináu (Kishinev) on July 16, 1941, which was practically without enemy opposition (despite the which 1 R-2 was destroyed and 5 R-2 damaged). They continued their pressure against the enemy until they reached Tighina on July 19 (losing 3 R-2 during the clashes). The campaign in Bessarabia finally ended on July 26, with the astonishing success of the Axis troops. Until then and despite the relativci̯ weak Soviet resistance, practically the Division could only count as still operational with half of its vehicles. This wear was motivated by the Soviets, but mainly by mechanical failures typical of the intense wear suffered in combats and by the usual organizational failures. After the combats, evaluating the activity of the 1st Romanian Armored Division during the Bessarabia campaign, it would be necessary to conclude that it had behaved properly (following the Romanian armored tactics) and had positively fulfilled the mission of attacking the flanks of the enemy. In addition the Soviet armored forces with which they had to face were still endowed by obsolete models of armored as the BT-2, BT-5, BT-7, T-26, T-37 and T-38.

The situation was so difficult, that the 1st Armored Division had to be out of service for ten days to try to put their vehicles in operational conditions again (let's think that since there were no repair vehicles either, everything became an exercise of patience and pure craftsmanship). It happened that some R-2 battered that could not be repaired "in situ" so they had to be moved to Bucharest or Ploiești to try to repair them in their country. This fact clearly shows us the limited operational capacity that could be expected from the Division.

As an interesting fact, in spite of the initial German intentions of not to make them coincide geographically in the front to Romanian and Hungarian troops. Despite this, on July 28, in the only case in which Romanian troops were on the flank of Magyar troops, the 3rd Calarasi Regiment of the 8th Romanian Cavalry Brigade withdrew before the first Soviet attack they received; consequently leaving the Hungarian right flank in danger. To avoid greater evils, that hole that was left un its right side was covered by the Hungarians themselves who finally managed in the fighting to take the town of Versad, in the vicinity of Gordiyevka.

Although we have focused on the 1st Armored Division, we must remember that the 1st Cavalry Brigade that also participated in the attack against the USSR, had 6 R-1 in its arsenal. These vehicles were used in reconnaissance tasks and in support of the troops.

The morale among the Romanian troops had been high during the campaign for Bessarabia and Northern Bukovina, but when orders were received to continue the advance into the USSR the unrest began among many of the Romanian soldiers as we shall read below.

The Odessa Siege

The Romanian people were happy with the result of the intervention of their Army in the conquest of Bessarabia, but this situation would change a few days later. On July 27, 1941, Hitler sent a letter to Antonescu, requesting Romanian collaboration for the capture of the city of Odessa. Romania accepted the requests of Germany, carrying the weight of the fighting for 73 days in what has come to be called the Odessa site. The intention of the Romanian High Command was to capture the city between August 10 and 15; we can see how the reality was very different.

On August 3, the 4th Romanian Army crossed the Dnestr River; on August 8, following Operational Directive No. 31, the Romanian High Command assigned the Romanian 4th Army the mission of defeating the Soviets between the Dnestr River and the Tiligulskiy area, and immediately afterwards headed for the city of Odessa. The armored support of the Romanian infantry troops was considered essential; so that the remains of the Armored Division after the combats of the previous days were put back in service towards the beginning of August. On the night between August 5 and 6, the Romanian 1st Armored Division crossed the Dnestr River, being subordinated to the Romanian V Corps and with the mission of heading towards the Black Sea coast to attack the defenders of Odessa from the flank. Thanks to the tactical support of the armored vehicles, it was initially considered that Odessa (and its strategic port) would be captured in just a few days, despite being powerfully defended by the Soviets.

Basically the assault on the city of Odessa turned out to be a real carnage since three well-protected defensive lines plenty of fortifications had been built and planted with anti-tank trenches, machine gun places, pillboxes, etc; likewise, in order to harden the conditions further, lands had been flooded to make it more difficult for the Axis troops to enter the city. With respect to the defensive lines, the first was about 140 kilometers long and was about 25-30 kilometers from the city (from the Adzhalikskiy estuary to the eastern coast of the Dnetrovskiy estuary), the second was about 8-15 kilometers away and stretched for about 80 kilometers (from Chebanka-Staraya to the east coast of the Sukhoy estuary) and the third was in the vicinity of the city (from Kryzhanovki to Lustford, in the last 8 kilometers and with about 40 kilometers of extension).

Another of the key elements in the defense of the city was the Soviet Black Sea Fleet, which provided support with its heavy-caliber weapons without the efforts of the Axis to subdue it could be carried out. The Soviets also counted on some armored vehicles for the defense of the city. It is calculated (according to Cloutier) that in August 1941, they had in Odessa at least 17 T-26 and 7 BT, in addition to another 26 tanks under repair in the same city (out of which 16 would be able to put in conditions to fight). It would be necessary for these tanks to finally add to other armored vehicles that they managed to gather in the city as the Soviet troops were retiring, between 70 and 120 (according to Axworthy) STZ tractors to which a 37 mm cannon was added or machine guns and four armored trains.

The imposing defenses and troops in Odessa, further delayed the Romanian advance, which had to travel with mud to advance their heavier guns. To such an extent did the difficulty to advance, that the 15th Infantry Division and the remains of the 1st Armored Division had to attack the Soviets without any support or prior recognition (which further increased their losses).

The intention of the 4th Romanian Army was to attack in a pincer movement with two formations: the III Corps and the V Corps. The III Corps composed of the 1st Division of the guard, the 3rd and 7th Infantry Divisions and the 2nd Regiment of the Armored Division (composed of the R-35) was to carry out an attack in the Razdelnaya-Odessa direction; on the other hand the V Corps was composed by the 1st Cavalry Brigade, 15th Infantry Division and the 1st Armored Division Regiment (composed of the R-2) that would carry out an attack in the direction of Katargy and Bol. Buzhalyk. Note that the cavalry units had some R-1 as reconnaissance and support vehicles.

Despite the numerical advantage of the Romanian troops (who acted with evident lack of coordination due to their bad radio communications), the Soviet defenders (two infantry Regiments, of which one was composed of sailors without previous training) managed to make them pay a high price for each step that progressed.

Detailing more painfully the arduous advance of the Romanian 1st Armored Division towards Odessa, on August 10 it managed to reach the population of Bol. Buzhalyk (still in the first Soviet defensive line) expelling the Soviets from there. At sunset on the same day, the vanguard of the 1st Division managed to reach the second defensive line by Blagodatnaya-Mal.Adzhalyk; for shortly after to be reinforced with the troops of the 1st Romanian Cavalry Division. After a brief rest, between August 11 and 12 the 1st Armored Division continued its advance towards Gildendorf (Svitle), in the vicinity of the Kuyalnitsky estuary. In this area, in addition to the Soviet troops, heavy rains and mud caused that only in those two days, 13 Romanian tanks were out of service (although they could recover in a couple of days). The same day, August 12, in the advance towards the railroad Razdelnaya-Odessa, at least other 5 Romanian tanks were destroyed when realizing the cover of another attack carried out by the Romanian infants.

Due to the high number of casualties on the Romanian side, on August 13 General Ion Antonescu decided to temporarily stop the offensive. But that did not end the suffering of the Romanians, both a Soviet counterattack northeast of Mannheim that was stopped by the Romanians, and in the fighting that the tanks of the 1st Armored Division were involved in the Buyalik area, where according Cloutier Romanian lost 9 R-2.

On the 14th, new clashes with the Soviets, according to Axworthy and Cloutier, ended with the loss of 25 more tanks. The fighting had become a continuous drain of men and vehicles on the Romanian side. Every meter the Romanians advanced, the Soviets made them pay a heavy cost. An example of this is what happened on the 16th at dusk, when an action of the Romanian infantry supported by 9 R-1 concluded with the defeat and withdrawal of the Soviet defenders in exchange for a good number of casualties in the troop and the loss of 4 R-1.

The advance was very hard for the Romanian tanks; summarizing the losses in the Romanian armored unit were distributed in this way: on August 11 they were out of combat 5 R-2, on the 12th they were 8 R-2, on August 13th 9 R-2 and on ugust 14th 25 R-2. Many of the R-2 had been involved in Soviet attacks in which they used Molotov cocktails and artillery (the poor coordination of the Romanian tanks with the own infantry troops was the cause in many cases of such a high number of losses). In three combat days, the 1st Armored Division had lost 47 R-2, so it was thought to remove it from the battle front. But before retreating to the remains of the Armored Division, another new attempt to cross the iron defenses of Odessa by the Romanian troops, ended up in a new disaster with numerous casualties (the Soviets knew about the supposed Romanian surprise attack from another different direction, so they had time to prepare their artillery to shoot on the attackers a heavy fire). Again the Romanian battle tanks acted separately, losing the theoretical firepower and advance they would have shown to act together.

On August 18 the day was witnessed with multiple clashes between Romanians and Soviet defenders. Before dawn, Romanian troops supported by armored vehicles of the Romanian Armored Division 1st Regiment participated in the fighting for the population of Kagarlik, as well as for the capture of the railway station of Karpovo (we have to remember the strategic importance of the Razdelnaya-Odessa line). Again, and continuing with the doctrine of the Romanian armored forces, the tanks did not act like an independent unit, but they were distributed between the troops of infantry to which they gave support and coverage. Again the result can be considered as a real disaster, because the cooperation with the infantry was not adequate since they were behind the tanks, being exposed the tanks to the 76.2 mm artillery and 45 mm anti-tank fire from the enemy that managed to knock out 32 Romanian tanks (11 destroyed and 24 damaged according to Axworthy). After this, the Romanians had to retreat at first, and later try again to progress against the enemy, in this case several Romanian R-2 moved towards the town of Vinogradar again without the proper support of the infantry. The story was repeated only a few hours later, and the Romanian tanks were again attacked with intense fire by the Soviets, who destroyed 3 R-2. After this new setback, the remaining R-2 had to be withdrawn before the imminent danger of being completely destroyed the Romanian armored unit. Despite the numerous casualties, the still available R-2 were again used in a new attack on the Karpovo railway station in conjunction with infantry troops, which was finally taken by the Romanian 11th Infantry Division.

In the so-called "Karpovo disaster", in addition to a large number of deaths, the Romanians in a single day had lost 35 R-2. The 1st Romanian Armored Division 1st Regiment had been left with only about 20 R-2 operatives (of the 105 that it counted at the beginning of the combats by Odessa). As many of them had been recovered, on August 21 the recovery services decided to send 46 damaged R-2s to Chisináu to try to repair them.

Meanwhile the 2nd Regiment of the Romanian armored division composed of 74 of the obsolete R-35, continued active in the fighting for Odessa although with a very limited strategic value (in spite of which and thanks to its thick armoring it provided them with a acceptable value in frontal assaults). As we discussed, from August 12 they were used in several attacks against the Soviets in the western area of the Dnestr River.

The real fact is that since the last week of August 1941, out of more than 100 R-2 with which the Armored Division counted, there were only 20 in service (one Battalion). The poor organization of the Romanian attack on Odessa, underestimating the Soviet defenders and the disastrous coordination between tanks and the infantry, had led to the fact that the Armored Division couldn´t be called as such because its losses. In the advance towards Freydental with its subsequent capture between the days 20 and 24, then from August 28, the Romanian tanks returned to take part in new combats (since the day of Karpovo they had not returned to be sent to combat). For this reason it was decided on the 26th, that the remains of the 1st Armored Division were grouped in a formation called "Lieutenant Colonel Eftimiu" Mechanized Detachment. This unit only had about 20 R-2 (10 according to other sources, although less credible), one Vanatori Motorized Battalion, one 105 mm Schneider Model 1936 Battalion, one 100 mm Škoda howitzer Battalion, one Engineers Company, a Gustloff 20 mm model 1938 anti-aircraft guns, one battery of 37 mm model 1939 anti-aircraft Rheinmetall guns and one Company with 12 47 mm model 1936 Schneider anti-tank guns. Apparently it was a good armored unit, although they were nothing more than the weak remains of the Romanian 1st Armored Division.

The "Lieutenant Colonel Eftimiu" Mechanized Detachment took part in the combats at the end of August and the first days of September framed in the XI Corps (which together with the I Corps, IV Corps and I Reserve Corps, constituted the 4th Romanian Army). In its advance, on August 31, the "Lieutenant Colonel Eftimiu" Mechanized Detachment lost 11 tanks in the fighting for the capture of Dalnik. Between Dalnik and Tatarka, the Detachment would be used again in support of the infantry in the first days of September, although at this point the number of troops had been reduced in great quantity. On September 14 we have again reports that placed the Detachment in the territory west of the Sukhoy estuary, as well as on days 16 and 17, in which the "Lieutenant Colonel Eftimiu" Mechanized Detachment was part of a German group. Romanian charged with assaulting the Soviet defenses. The attack against Odessa persisted, so that on September 17 the Romanian troops that remained active in union with German troops, charged against the second defensive ring of the fenced city. Again this attempt ended up in failure due to the strong resistance offered by the Soviets.

On September 20, the "Lieutenant Colonel Eftimiu" Mechanized Detachment received some vehicles in combat conditions. The so-called 1st Assault Detachment was formed with all of them, consisting of 12 R-2 and 10 R-35.

Between September 24th and October 1st, by orders of Antonescu, the 4th Romanian Army suspended its offensive maneuvers against Odessa, limiting itself only to respond before attacks of the Soviets. This period was used to reorganize the depleted Romanian troops. As for the "Lieutenant Colonel Eftimiu", Mechanized Detachment this was included in the IV Corps.

It was not until mid-October on October 16, 1941 that the city of Odessa finally fell into the hands of Romanian 4th Army after the Soviet defenders were evacuated (mainly because of the inability of the Soviets to keep the city in their hands) thanks to the intervention of Soviet Navy. It was at 11.00 a.m. on October 16 when the Romanian troops noticed that the Soviets had evacuated their defenses and fled (at 05.10 a.m. in the same day, the Soviet troops HQ in Odessa had been evacuated). At 16.00, already inside an abandoned city (it really was not completely since 7000 Soviet soldiers were captured, apart from the civilian population that amounted to 220000 people), the remains of the Mechanized Detachment "Lieutenant Colonel Eftimiu" took the harbour of the city. A great victory for Romania that tried to increase its importance within the Axis, but the other side of the victory was the practical dismantling of the 1st Armored Division and of course of some 70000-100000 casualties.

The Mechanized Detachment "Lieutenant Colonel Eftimiu" as we have seen was the armored unit that would take part in the siege of Odessa until it was captured, after which the Detachment was dissolved. The formation of detachments that grouped the armored in active service after having been decimated an armored unit became a fact that sadly was repeated in more than one occasion during the Romanian intervention in World War II.

During the bloody battles over the capture of Odessa, some of the Romanian tank commanders stood out, such as Captain Octavian Miclescu (born in 1909 in Roman and then head of an R-2 Company of the 1st Tank Regiment) that with his Company faced a Soviet motorized column in retreat towards Zhiminova. In the tough confrontation that followed, Captain Octavian Miclescu was wounded in the shoulder, but managed to capture 10 cars and make 170 prisoners. In this action Octavian Miclescu earned the award Steaua Romaniei with Virtute Militara.

The disaster of the Armored Division in the combats by Odessa later had important repercussions in the organization and deployment of the Axis troops in Soviet territory. Thus the 1st Armored Division, could not join the 3rd Romanian Army in Ukraine (a fact that crucially weakened the Army Group South) and that would later suffer the consequences before the growing Sovietarmored power.

At the end of October 1941, the 1st Armored Division was in a very bad situation so it became necessary to transfer it to Romania in order to be repaired, resupplied, re-trained and reorganized (it needed more than 10 months to reacquire combat capacity again). In fact, after evaluating the obsolete tank R-35 in combat, the 1st Armored Division 2nd Regiment with the R-35 still in service, were sent to Romania, being relegated to a training role.

This fact would leave the Romanians at the front without their own armored support, so Germany was asked for permission to acquire tanks for the Škoda company. The initial number of battle tanks requested amounted to 26 Pz.35 (the LT-35, which at the time were very similar to the R-2) and would come from the German reserves (they had previously served with the 11th Panzer Division) since these were the ones who managed the armament industries in the former Czechoslovakia. These tanks had been in service on the front line with the Germans, so they required adequate preparation to put them back into service. This motivated that they were only ready to be sent to Rumania in May 1942, and to be more exact, these arrived at Romanian territory between June and July 1942. Due to this enormous delay in the acquisition of those tanks, Romania tried to obtain other tanks in other ways. Romania before its entry into the world conflict, had tried again to increase the number of armored vehicles in his Army. As early as January 1941 there were contacts (authorized by the Wehrmacht) between the Romanian Army and the war industries of the former Czechoslovakia. It was Colonel Constantin Ghiulai who negotiated in the dismembered Czechoslovakia, the acquisition of the T-23M battle tank and the TNH for its production under license by the Reşiţa facilities in Bucharest to replace the R-1 tanks. With this, they wanted to re-equip the Cavalry units with an armored vehicle with high performance(in October 1941, all the R-1 tanks had been put out of action, although some of them could be repaired later). But these negotiations were not successful, so they had to enter in 1942 with the remains that they still managed to keep in service of their Armored Forces.

During the year 1941 the Romanian Armored Forces were decimated; thus the 1st Tank Regiment lost 26 R-2 and 60 R-2 tanks were badly damaged, and only a few tanks managed to escape slightly damaged with consequent wear. The 2nd Tank Regiment lost 15 R-35, another 25 of them were severely damaged (despite their obsolescence on a date like 1941, at least their crews did appreciate the thick armor that these tanks of French origin had). To worsen the balance, the Romanian tanks tactics were not adequate despite the bravery and will of the crews of the same. If it´s necessary to compare his attitude, it would not be less than that of his Soviet rivals or German friends, but Romania carried a significant burden consisting in the practical absence of an adequate enemy reconnaissance, very little ability to maintain and repair the damaged tanks, and as we have said, the wrong doctrine of the use of Armored Forces.

The final numbers of the 1st Armored Division after the 1941 campaign were disastrous due to the loss of: 111 tanks, 206 vehicles of various types; as well as 34 officers, 102 non-commissioned officers, 1125 soldiers, 463 rifles, 54 light machine guns, and 5 heavy machine guns.

A Romanian Schneider anti-tank gun team during the clashes against the Soviets in October 1941. The small caliber of the Romanian anti-tank guns was very unsuccessfull against Soviet modern tanks. [Courtesy by Pusca and Nitu from worldwar2.ro from MMN]

A Romanian armored column of R-2 tanks belonging to the Romanian 1st Armored Division drive along Soviet lands near near Odessa, 1941. In those combats, the R-2s were used as a support for the infantry, thanks to their 37 mm gun. [Courtesy by Pusca and Nitu from worldwar2.ro from Armata Romana 1941-1945]

Map of Romania 1942 with the new territories annexed to the USSR. In the picture you can see the Hungarian Transylvania almost splitting the country in two. [From public domain - by Anton Gutsunaev (changes by Rowanwindwhistler)]

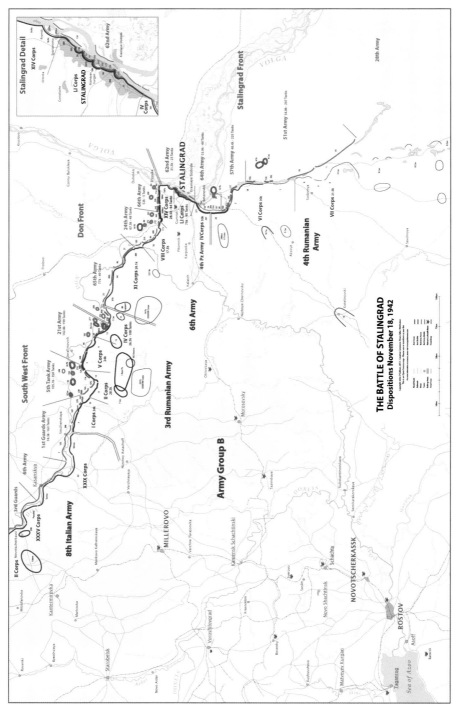

Axis Defensive line on the Don front and Stalingrad November 18, 1942. The 1st Romanian Armored Division is located in the upper center together with the 22nd Panzer Division in its rearguard as 3rd Romanian Army reserve units. [From public domain - by Josullivan.59]

Photograph of a T-4 (PzKpfw IV Ausf. J) exhibited at the National Military Museum in Bucharest. This type of tank represented the top of Romanian armored power during WW2.
[From public domain – by mircea87]

A T-4 moves through the field. The arrival of more than 100 tanks of this type, allowed the Romanian 1st Armored Division and some other units to significantly increase their firepower.
[From public domain]

Several TACAM T-60 during a parade possibly on May 10, 1943 in Bucharest. On January 12, 1943, a first TACAM T-60 prototype had already been manufactured, which was received with great acceptance due to its functional resemblance to the German Marder. [From public domain]

An American B-24 bomber overflies the oil fields of Ploiesti during a bombing on August 1, 1943. The Allied strategy of stopping the supply of Romanian fuel to Germany caused great damage after 1943 in the German Army. [From public domain]

Painted by Arkadiusz Wrobel

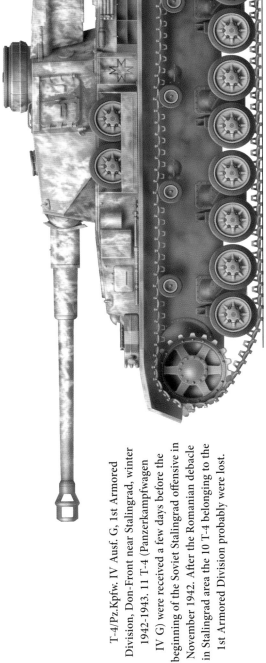

T-3/Pz.Kpfw. III Ausf. N, 1st Armored Division, Don-Front near Stalingrad, Winter 1942-43. On October 17, 1942 Germany agreed to deliver 11 Panzerkampfwagen III Ausf N equipped with a short 75 mm KwK L/24 low-speed gun. Immediately 10 T-3s were incorporated into the 1st Romanian Armored Division 1st Tank Regiment that was deployed in the Don river front.

T-4/Pz.Kpfw. IV Ausf. G, 1st Armored Division, Don-Front near Stalingrad, winter 1942-1943. 11 T-4 (Panzerkampfwagen IV G) were received a few days before the beginning of the Soviet Stalingrad offensive in November 1942. After the Romanian debacle in Stalingrad area the 10 T-4 belonging to the 1st Armored Division probably were lost.

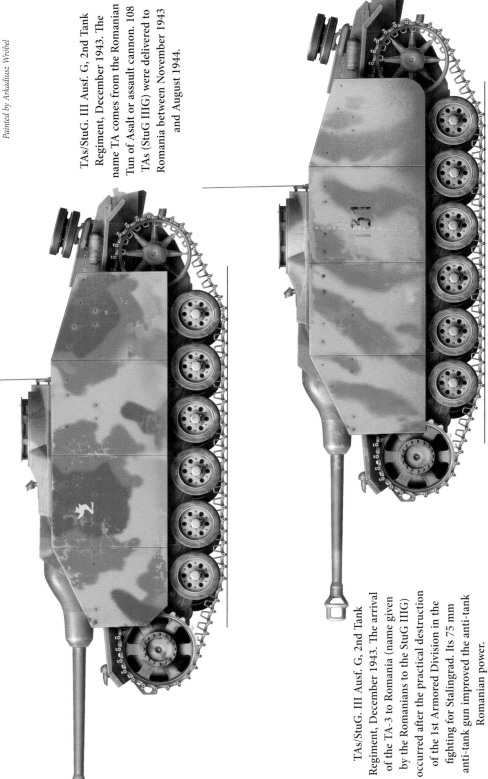

Painted by Arkadiusz Wróbel

TAs/StuG. III Ausf. G, 2nd Tank Regiment, December 1943. The name TA comes from the Romanian Tun of Asalt or assault cannon. 108 TAs (StuG IIIG) were delivered to Romania between November 1943 and August 1944.

TAs/StuG. III Ausf. G, 2nd Tank Regiment, December 1943. The arrival of the TA-3 to Romania (name given by the Romanians to the StuG IIIG) occurred after the practical destruction of the 1st Armored Division in the fighting for Stalingrad. Its 75 mm anti-tank gun improved the anti-tank Romanian power.

CHAPTER VI

1942. From Attack To Defense

Romania began the year 1942 with its Armored Forces being very weakened so that little could be expected of them from the operational point of view. The 1st Armored Division changed its chief, becoming General Major Radu Gherghe (he was in this position from January 11, 1942 to March 20, 1943). While it is true that the Crimean campaign lasted until July of that same year, the participation of Romanian armor was conspicuous by its absence during the first half of 1942. The Corneliu Dragalina´s VI Corps would direct its steps towards Stalingrad while the 3rd Army would continue towards the Caucasus subordinated to the 17th German Army with which it would arrive until the area near of Grozny between October and November of 1942 (although with these Romanian troops they did not serve armored units of the same nationality).

Stalingrad. The Annihilation Of 1st Armored Division.

Following the works of Nitu, Pusca, Axworthy, Cloutier, Zaloga, Joly and Filipescu, we will try to explain the almost destruction of the 1st Armored Division.

As we have said, during the summer Crimea ceased to be the main theater of Romanian operations since the bulk of the Romanian war activities (as well as its armored troops still in full period of reorganization with the replenishment of the severe losses sustained during the campaign of the previous year) was sent to the banks of the Don covering the flanks of the XI Army commanded by Paulus that was heading towards Stalingrad to take it for its strategic importance. Along with Romanians, Italian and Hungarian troops (these last traditional enemies of the Romanians) completed the network of Axis forces in this offensive that would become vital in the future evolution of the world conflict.

At the beginning of the year, they tried to put the Romanian tanks in the most optimal conditions so 40 R-2 were sent to the facilities of Škoda in Plzen (Pilzen) to be reviewed. Likewise, another 50 were sent to the Škoda workshops in Ploieşti for minor repairs.

Despite trying to improve the capabilities of the Romanian tanks, the Army knew the limitations of the R-2. It is known the fact of a test that made the Romanians to check the capacity of their armor against the Soviet tanks, in a test with real fire of the R-2 against a captured Soviet T-34. The result was disheartening as it was found that the effect of the 37 mm projectiles against the thick armor of the T-34 was practically zero even at short distances. On the other hand, the effect of the gun of the T-34 was devastating on the light armoring of the R-2 at any distance. This study led to the urgent request to Germany for new tanks that could destroy the powerful T-34.

Between June and July, the 26 Pz. 35 that Germany had agreed to sell to Romania were well received. These tanks were previously checked by Škoda and the low combat level of the Romanian Armored Forces improved very little.

During this period prior to the fighting for Stalingrad, the Romanian Army HQ was looking for new solutions to its important deficit in armored vehicles, taking into account the limitations of their national war industry. So they started working on a mixed armor based on the chassis of the Soviet T-60 with a 76.2 mm F22 cannon (also from the captured ones to the Soviets). They also began to work on a similar idea although using the chassis of the R-2 also with the F22 cannon (although due to the shortage of this weapon, they would finally choose the 76.2 mm Zis-3 of Soviet origin). In any case, these projects would not see the light until many months later, as we will explain later (the project based on the T-60 would wait until June 1943, and the one based on the R-2 until July 1944).

As we mentioned earlier, after the capture of Odessa, the 1st Armored Division had been sent to Romania to rebuild it as an operational Unit; for which they were necessary up to 10 months of hard work. In mid-1942, the Romanian High Command considered it could be sent back to the front. It was decided that the 1st Armored Division along with some other units also rebuilt were assigned to the 3rd Romanian Army in its advance through the southern USSR. It was necessary to wait until September 1942 to be transferred to the Eastern Front, although the 1st Armored Division would not be operational again until October 17, 1942; it was finally reorganized thanks to the incorporation of new armored material from Germany. The panorama that the Romanians had to face, with the obsolete battle tanks that they had available to fight the increasingly powerful Soviet armored forces, motivated the Romanian government to request new tanks for the Germans again. In this occasion the Romanian request was attended, reason by which little more than a twenty of new battle tanks were transferred from German arsenals. These tanks were from types more powerful to any tank type that Romania had put until that moment in service; we refer to 11 Pz. IIIN (denominated in Romania as T3) and to 11 Pz. IVG (now referred to as T4). These tanks were incorporated into the 1st Armored Division 1st Tank Regiment, automatically becoming the spearhead of the 1st Romanian Armored Division. Thanks to this new incorporation of modern tanks, the 1st Armored Division finally acquired a certain capacity to face its Soviet rivals (although we must remember that the commissioning of the new tanks was not immediate, so that in November 19, only 19 of the 22 tanks were available, although it is true that a copy of the T-3 and another of the T-4 were sent to Romania to be dedicated to training new crews in these new tanks). According to Axworthy, at that time the Division had 2 Soviet tanks captured in service, one of 7 and another of 12 tons. The Romanian unit was also reinforced with the necessary artillery guns to enhance its anti-tank capacity, with 9 50 mm Pak 38 and 9 75 mm Pak 40 with their corresponding Zugkraftwagen tractors. Finally the motorized Division reconnaissance troops were strengthened with several Sdkfz 222 (6) and Sdkfz 223 (5).

So the rebuilt 1st Armored Division was in October as follows:

- 1st Tank Regiment.
- 3rd Motorized Vanatori Regiment.
- 4th Motorized Vanatori Regiment.
- 1st Motorized Artillery Regiment.
- Special Weapons Motorized Group.
- Reconnaissance Motorized Group.
- Motorized Engineers Battalion.
- Anti-tank Battalion.
- Antiaircraft Company.
- Communications Company.
- Services Group.
- Traffic Squad.
- Police Company.

The most powerful unit of the Division was its 1st Tank Regiment, which was constituted by two Battalions made up of four Companies, 3 of them being of tanks R-2 and the fourth was a Company of medium tanks (the T-4 were assigned to the 1st Battalion 4th Company and the T-3 to the 2nd Battalion 8th Company). These two companies were endowed with the T3 and T-4, the only ones that really had the capacity to face their Soviet rivals with efficiency; since the Companies equipped with the R-2 were not at all a rival for the T-34 and other enemy armor, as had already been shown only a few months before.

They were attached to Army Group B commanded by Marshal von Bock, the 4th Panzer Army, part of the 2nd Hungarian Army, the 2nd and 6th German Armies and the 3rd Romanian Army; with the mission to support the left wing of the German advance towards Stalingrad. This Army Group along with the Army Group A, would be the main actors in the Blue Case (the German plan of operations for the summer of 1942 that was developed in the southern zone of the Eastern Front).

The operational force available to the Division just before the operations aimed at the Stalingrad takeover were initiated was as follows:

- 501 officers.
- 538 NCOs.
- 11,592 soldiers.
- 9,335 rifles.
- 278 light machine guns.
- 61 heavy machine guns.
- 67 mortars.
- 36 cannons and howitzers.
- 1,358 vehicles.
- 109 R-2.
- 11 T-3.
- 11 T-4.
- 2 captured Soviet tanks (possibly a T-60 and a BT-7).
- 10 AB armored vehicles (Sdkfz 222). Posibly adquired after Soviet attack started.
- 8 armored personnel carriers (SPW 251). Posibly adquired after Soviet attack started.

After the expected reorganization of fall in 1942, the Division became operative so it was immediately called upon to participate in the operations aimed to taking Stalingrad to support the Romanian troops that were already there. The Division was subordinated to the 48th German Panzer Corps (under the command of Lieutenant General Ferdinand Heim) as were the 22nd German Panzer Division and parts of the 14th Panzer Division. The total number of tanks in the 48th Panzer Corps reached 255 units. Out of them, approximately one half were Romanian. There is different information on the maintenance status of the tanks of the 22nd Panzer Division that coincides in the fact that being in positions of defense covered with straw to protect from the cold for a long time would cause a large number of mice sought shelter and heat in the tanks. Specifically the mice occupied the areas that generated more heat such as motors and electrical wiring systems, deteriorating them completely together with the parts where there were rubber structures (to this fact we must add the chronic shortage of spare parts that would solve the problem). In fact when they tried to start the 22nd Panzer Division Pz. 38s, only (according to Beevor) around 30 tanks were still able to be used, which corresponds to 1/3 of the 104 that the Unit should have. It is necessary to add that the 22nd Panzer Division had not been modernized with new tanks as had happened in other German units.

The matter of the mice was not discovered previously due to the little reserve of fuel with which the 22nd Panzer Division counted, which limited the use of them to the minimum despite the complaints of the crews and mechanics. The critical fuel level of the Germans reached such a point that they had to use part of the fuel reserves of the Romanian 1st Armored Division.

In front of them the main force that opposed the Romanian troops was the men of the Soviet South-West Front that had a large number of T-34 and KV as well as a large number of light tanks such as the T-60. The most powerful unit of this Soviet Group was the 5th Armored Army that included the 1st and 26th Armored Corps; very tough rivals for the general obsolescence that 48th Panzer Corps tanks had.

In September 1942 the 3rd and 4th Romanian Armies began to take positions on the flanks of the city of Stalingrad (after its conquest Hitler had planned that together with the German Sixth Army, these Romanian Armies would form Mariscal Antonescu Army Group to carry out operations east of the Volga River, as well as ground troops, also Romanian Air Force forces, would also take part in the war actions in Stalingrad). The 3rd Romanian Army commanded by General Petre Dumitrescu was transferred from the Caucasus, being entrusted with a front line between Lugovsky and Sukhoidonetz that covered about 138 kilometers, well above the operational capacity of the Army. In addition, the Soviets had two bridgeheads across the Donetz River, at Serafimovich and at Kleeskaya. Dumitrescu complained repeatedly of such a situation, requesting reinforcements or at least the elimination of those Soviet bridgeheads could be eliminated. At that time the 3rd Romanian Army was constituted by the IV Corps (that included the 13th Infantry Division and 1st Cavalry Division), V Corps (that included 5th and 6th Infantry Divisions), the II Corps (that included 9th and 14th Infantry Divisions), and the I Corps (that included 7th and 11th Infantry divisions). Once these troops were ready at the front, only the 15th Infantry and 7th Cavalry Divisions remained in reserve. The Soviet HQ was aware that the Romanians did not have any more reserves, so they were a priority objective. Similarly, the German HQ was also aware that Romanian defensive lines could hardly withstand a massive Soviet attack.

After the expected reorganization of fall of 1942, the Romanian 1st Armored Division became operative thanks to the fact that it had been equipped with more modern battle tanks (in addition to the obsolete Pz.35 (t) or R-2). After receiving a brief joint training with German troops near Doneck, it was immediately called upon to participate in the operations aimed at taking Stalingrad to support the Romanian troops who were already there (only during the journey they traveled to join their German comrades were lost 12 R-2 tanks without any contact with enemy troops). In fact the regrettable state of some of the R-2 motivated that 35 of them did not accompany the rest of the Division to the front of combat and they were kept in deposits before crossing the Chir River.

On October 9 the Romanian Armored Division joined the 6th German Army near Chernychevska, which was already preparing for the assault on the city of Stalingrad; leaving the Division subordinated to the 48th German Panzer Corps. In November the 48th German Panzer Corps was composed of the 22nd Panzer Division and the 1st Romanian Armored Division that were behind the 3rd Romanian Army, as a reserve. This German Panzer Corps also had other units such as the 2nd, 4th, 5th and 8th heavy motorized Artillery Regiments; as well as the 41st independent motorized heavy Artillery Battalion. At that time they only had 48 heavy anti-tank guns for the entire 3rd Romanian Army (which at that time was the only one that was useful against the feared Soviet T-34 and KV). While the 6th German Army carried most of the effort for the capture of Stalingrad, the 3rd Romanian Army positioned itself on its left flank to the west along the Don River. In that area there was a Soviet bridgehead south of Kremenskaya, which became a major problem for the defenders in a short time.

The training of the crews of the newcomers T-3 and T-4 within the 1st Armored Division could not be very good since by mid-November 1942 the Soviets would carry out a counter-offensive that would end the training. Immediately before the Soviet offensive, the 1st Armored Division was in the vicinity of Perelazovskij and Petrovka to cross the Chir River and had service at 84 R-2, 19 T3 and T4 and a pair of captured Soviet tanks. The distribution within the 1st Armored Division was in three Combat Groups: "Coronel Pastia" Group, "Coronel Nistor" Group and "Otto Benedict" Reconnaissance Group.

On November 19, 1942 when the Soviets began their winter offensive (Operation Uranus), the 3rd Romanian Army had 152492 Romanians and 11211 Germans. For its part, the 4th Romanian Army commanded by General Constantin Contanstinescu occupied a front line south of Stalingrad between Straya Otrada and Sarta. The 4th Romanian Army was constituted by the VI Corps (with the Infantry Divisions 1st, 2nd, 4th, 18th and 20th) and the VII Corps (with the 5th and 8th Cavalry Divisions), also counting with Romanian and German air support. On paper, the front lines of the 4th Romanian Army covered 270 kilometers, but its extension was actually more than 300 kilometers, motivated by the difficult of orography. This fact motivated the Romanian troops to extend themselves far more than was reasonable (a fact that would later have its negative consequences during the Soviet offensive). Another problem of the Romanian troops was the operational level of their units, since they were far from 100% of their operational capacity, being mainly between 50-75% and slightly less than 50% (the only exception being the 1st Romanian Infantry Division that was 25%). In addition, the little affinity of Romanian soldiers for their officers, didn´t work to improve the Romanian defensive capacity. On the left flank of the 4th Romanian Army was the 29th German Motorized Infantry Division, which would be ready to support the Romanians if necessary. In reference to the number of anti-tank guns in the 4th Army, we found again that it was very limited, with an anti-tank gun for every 5.7 kilometers in front. The number of men was 75580 (before the Soviet offensive).

The 3rd and 4th Romanian Armies were not united in the front, but instead they were arranged among them the German Sixth Army commanded by General

Friedrich Von Paulus (in Stalingrad), as well as part of the 4th Panzer Army. Also on the front line were the 8th Italian Army and the 2nd Hungarian Army. All these Armies (3rd and 4th Romanian Armies, 6th German Army, 4th Panzer Army, 8th Italian Army and 2nd Hungarian Army) formed Army Group B.

The enemies arranged against the Romanian 3rd Army were those of the aforementioned Soviet South-Western Front, composed of the 1st Guard Army, 5th Armored Army and the 21st Army. This Soviet South-Western Front had 728 tanks, 790 aircraft and 5888 artillery pieces. In front of the 4th Romanian Army were the units of the Stalingrad front with the 57th, 51st, 62nd and 63rd Armies, which had 455 tanks, air support and 4931 artillery pieces. Obviously the 3rd and 4th Romanian armies were completely overcome by their opponents.

According to reports from the Romanian 3rd Army itself, on November 17 they had executed only 60-70% of the trenches, 20-30% of the fences and 30-40% of the minefields that were planned to be deployed on the line head on. It was a clear example of the poor defensive preparation that could be planted against the Soviets just a couple of days later.

As we have said, Operation Uranus was unleashed on November 19 at 5:30 AM, which was the moment in which the offensive began with a violent artillery bombing hit the sector of the Romanian 3rd Army (the second defensive line was the most damaged, since it was how the Soviets paralyzed the possibility of the arrival of new reinforcements from the rear). The Romanian 1st Armored Division was deployed in the Perelasovskiy area and the 22nd Panzer Division in the Chernashevskaya area. At that time the weather conditions with blizzard, snow and temperatures below 20 degrees Celsius were extreme for attackers and defenders. Despite this, the Soviet Army under the command of Rokossovsky departing from the Kramenskaya bridgehead began his attack without mercy, hitting the Romanian units and breaking their defensive system. Elements of the 51st Soviet Armored Army began the offensive, attacking the positions of the 14th Romanian Infantry Division; while the 21st Soviet Army attacked the positions of the 1st Cavalry Division and the 13th Romanian Infantry Division. In general, except for the few heavy anti-tank guns, the bulk of the Romanian artillery, which was constituted mainly by pieces of small caliber (37 or 47 mm) against which the T-34 were practically invulnerable, could do little against the Soviets. Despite the debacle that loomed over the Romanians, they tried to defend themselves and resist as much as possible in their positions to later retreat but without managing to distance their troops in retreat from the Soviet outposts. Thanks to the courageous behavior of the Romanian soldiers they managed at least to stop sometime the Soviet attack, even destroying some tanks (in the front area of the 13th Romanian Division the defenders managed to destroy 25 Soviet tanks of the Red Army first wave although finally the Soviets managed to overtake the Romanian fleeing troops, getting close to them.

The commanding general of the 48th Panzer Corps, at 5.50 am, was aware of the massive Soviet attack, and ordered that reconnaissance missions be carried out in the Kletskaya and Bolshoyie areas. After receiving the reports from his reconnaissance troops and without any specific authorization from the Army Group HQ, he decided to send the 48th Panzer Corps northeast to stop the Soviet advance on Kletskaia with a counterattack. So at 10.00 AM the order was given for the 1st Romanian Armored Division and the 22nd Panzer Division (and a Kampfgruppe Group of the 14th Panzer Division) to head towards Kletskaia, along with the 7th Cavalry Division to try to tackle the Soviet onslaught. But the confusion of the moment, together with the hesitant orders of Adolf Hitler, determined that at 11.30 AM, the Romanian and German armor were redirected to the northwest. The problem was that bad communications prevented the 1st Romanian Division from receiving this countermand and continued fulfilling the previous orders. As a result of this fact, the Romanian 1st Armored Division was overtaken by the Soviet outposts among which was the 26th Armored Corps (with which the Romanian armored vehicles were mixed) that tried to "clean" the area north of Perelasovskiy, submerging the Romanians in a real chaos despite which they tried to move from Perelasovskiy towards Serafimovich. To the critical of the situation it had to be added that once the Romanian 1st Armored Division was isolated, it also had no possibility of refueling, which limited the Romanian fighting capacity even more.

On the first day of the offensive, the enemy succeeded in creating two breaches in the defensive line of the 3rd Romanian Army. One located in the center of the lines of the 3rd Romanian Army, with 16-18 kilometers in width and with a depth of 15 kilometers, being the other breach achieved in the right wing (between the 3rd Romanian Army and the 6th German Army) with 10-12 kilometers wide with a depth of 35-40 kilometers.

During the first day of the offensive, casualties on both sides were very high in human lives and in battle tanks (62 lost by the Soviets at the hands of the Romanians, while the Romanians themselves lost 25 of their own tanks).

On November 20 the Soviet armored troops advanced towards Kalach with the intention of encircling the VI German Army that was fighting in Stalingrad (during the night between the 20th and the 21st General Major Rodin ordered to advance the 19th Tank Brigade and take the Kalach bridge). Also, the 22nd Panzer Division, surpassed in Petshany by numerous Soviet armored forces, had to withdraw to the north of Bol.Donschynka (Bolshaya Donschynka), while facing the armored 1st Armored Corps. The radio station that used the Romanian 1st Armored Division to communicate with the Germans, as was destroyed in this night attack (the Soviet forces of the 1st Armored Corps surpassed the Romanian HQ in Shirk where the radio station was located despite the Romanian resistance), made communication with its allies impossible and therefore the coordination of its armor with those of the Germans for defense. Despite this, the situation was very clear; the Romanian 1st Armored Division should try to link with the 22nd German Panzer Division in Petshany, so the Romanians were ordered to attack on the morning of November 20 to capture the highs in southern of Teich. However the Romanian 1st Armored Division only managed initially to advance a few kilometers west of Korotovsky, as the Soviets carried out numerous counterattacks by Soviet mechanized forces (the rival of the Romanians was the 19th Soviet Tank Brigade, belonging to the 26th Armored Corps) that finally slowed it down (the Romanian 1st Armored Division had managed to establish a small bridgehead west of the Zariza River, but failed to contact the Germans). At least the tenacious resistance of the Romanians prevented a complete break of the front by the Soviets from the start. The Soviet tanks were now among the armored vehicles belonging to the 22nd German Panzer Division and the 1st Romanian Armored Division. Since the Soviets were penetrating more and more kilometers inside the defensive lines, they managed to surround the V Army Corps. At three o'clock in the afternoon in the sector of the IV Army Corps, 40 Soviet tanks attacked the area of the 15th Infantry Division, which lacked heavy antitank could not withstand the enemy's attack, being annihilated. The 1st Romanian Cavalry Division with its handful of R-1, in its withdrawal went to Stalingrad being incorporated into the VI Army.

During day 20, one of the most important fights in which the Romanian 1st Armored Division was involved was the counterattack against the Winterlager farm. This farm was in the path that the Romanian division had to follow to try to connect with the 22nd German Panzer Division and it was already occupied by important Soviet forces that became strong in the position.

The main part of the Romanian attack was carried by the battle tanks of German origin possessed by the Romanians: the T-3 (Pz III) and T-4 (Pz IV); although also the R-2 (Pz. 35 (t)) must have given their best. The Romanian forces during the counterattack against the Soviet positions successfully tried to reach the existing heights in the vicinity of the farm by using the Pz tanks. 35 (t) belonging to the 1st Armored Regiment 7th Company as spearhead. Simultaneously the medium tanks belonging to the 1st Armored Regiment 8th Company supported among others by the Pz. 35 (t) belonging to the 1st Armored Regiment 3rd Company tried to break the enemy's resistance in order to continue the advance to their motorized troops (the Vanatori). During this Romanian action there were several Romanian tankers who in their Pz. III and Pz. 35 (t) risked their lives in continuous attacks until they finally managed to break the resistance of the defenders. But that small success was continued by a Soviet counterattack with tanks at dusk so the Romanian tanks fought until they ran out of ammunition. Finally the Romanians achieved their goals and "cleaned" the road to continue their painful advance behind the enemy lines. That day and the coming days, several tanks leaders showed their bravery in the combats as the captain Constantin Neagu from 3rd Company, Sergeant Major Stefan Raducu from 4th Company, Captain Ioan Chifulescu from 7th Company, Sergeant Alexandru Velican, Second Lieutenant Gheorghe Budu Florea and Captain Parvanescu from 8th Company. The suffering and courage demonstrated in all the battles that the Romanian troops sustained were not finally rewarded at the end of the day, with the link to the 22nd Panzer Division.

For its part, the Romanian 3rd Army at the end of day 20, had a hole in the center of its lines over 70 kilometers wide; immediately behind this fracture of the Romanian lines, the Romanian 1st Armored Division was encircled. The 5th, 6th and 15th Infantry Divisions, as well as remnants of the 13th and 14th Infantry Divisions, were also surrounded very fast. In total the infantry troops in the pocket were some 40,000 men, who formed the so-called "General Lascar" Combat Group. Also, the Romanian 1st Armored Division had lost some 25 tanks but had managed to destroy 62 enemy tanks (according to Romanian sources).

The High Command of the 48th German Panzer Corps had considered it transcendental that the two armored forces (the 22nd German Panzer Division and the 1st Romanian Armored Division) had to be united to somehow increase their chances of survival on the battlefield.

On November 21st, the Romanian 1st Armored Division was pocketed along with the aforementioned Romanian units of the "General Lascar" Combat Group, completely surrounded by the Soviets; so it became a priority to try to join the rest of the Axis troops. For this reason, the Romanian 1st Armored Division (which was in the area of Nishne Zaritzya) was entrusted with the mission of fighting south-southwest towards the town of Perelasovski to cover the left flank of the 5th Division Infantry that was in the western heights in the Zaritzya valley. Also that same day November 21, the 22nd Panzer Division tried from its position Bol.Donschynka (within the defensive line of the Axis troops) move towards Perelasovski to achieve link with the 1st Romanian Armored Division and thus try to free the "General Lascar" Combat Group. This attempt failed as it was fully stopped on November 22 between Bol.Donschynka and Perelasovski. Not being able to continue advancing the 22nd Panzer Division, they decided to wait in Perelasovski to be the 1st Romanian armored Division to join her after getting away by their own means of the pocket in which they were (at this time, the 22nd Panzer Division ran the risk of being encircled also by the Soviet troops who continued their advance towards the river Chir). Meanwhile, from the dawn of November 22, the 1st Romanian Armored Division separated definitively from the rest of the units of the "General Lascar" Combat Group that remained behind, while it continued advancing slowly towards Bol.Donschynka, where they expected to meet with its German comrades who were waiting for them (by that time the few armored vehicles that remained working in 22nd Panzer Division had retreated from Perelasovski to more secure positions in the area of Bol.Donschynka). But this village, which the Romanian 1st Armored Division was trying to reach, was already under Soviet control; to which was added the lack of ammunition, food and fuel (it was already four days without any provisioning and the situation became very serious for the progress of the tanks). Faced with this situation that put the Division to the limit of its strength, the Romanians asked for air support radio to provide them with all the elements they needed to continue their advance. In spite of the difficulties, their calls by radio were attended and in a short time airplanes belonging to the 105th Transport Squadron provided them with ammunition, food and fuel thanks to an improvised runway. Thanks to this supply when the Romanian 1st Armored Division was practically with the engines turned off, they were able to continue its difficult advance towards the south with a view to meeting the 22nd Panzer Division but now with the fuel levels of its armored vehicles, again maximum. In their march towards the south, on November 22 near of the town of Bol.Donschynka they found a Soviet cavalry unit (possibly belonging to the 8th Soviet Cavalry Corps) that had the support of armored T-60 and T-70. The 112th Soviet Cavalry Division attacked in the vicinity of Bol.Donschynka against Romanian infantry troops supported by some 25 tanks of the Romanian 1st Armored Division. In these combats the tanks belonging to 1st Armored Regiment 7th Company did their work successfully, because they finally defeated their rivals without backing off their positions in Bol.Donschynka. Despite being decimated and exhausted, the men belonging to the 1st Romanian Armored Division tried in November 22 to break the siege in what the 22nd Panzer Division was within to try to join their German comrades. But the Soviet resistance was so tenacious that they were repulsed and forced to retreat while they continued fighting in the direction of Petrovka (where they arrived at dusk). The result of this attempt to break the siege was 2 tanks and at least another 59 vehicles destroyed. At the end of the day at least 10 Romanian tanks had been knocked out in exchange for destroying some 65 Soviet tanks.

On November 23, during the course of these retreating fighting, in the town of Ossinovsky, the 1st Romanian Armored Division 1st Tank Regiment 8th Tank Company (with its medium tanks) managed to stop the continuous attacks of Soviet cavalry units that had infiltrated after the men of the 3rd Motorized Vanatori Regiment, for seven hours. Also the retreating Romanians held combats in the areas of Oserski and Riabuhin; near Ossinovsky.

At this point and after only three days of combat, the 1st Armored Division was quite depleted in its potential, since it had 19 R-2, 11 T-3 and T-4 (some other tanks that were damaged or without fuel, were under tow); and these were generally quite damaged and short of fuel again. Despite the great effort made, contact with the "General Lascar" Combat Group had not been achieved, the latter having to finally reach the positions of the armored unit by their own means.

We report below the movements of this Combat Group destined to link with their compatriots who belonged to the 1st Armored Division. Let's go back to November 22, when the surviving part of the "General Lascar" Combat Group that remained surrounded, was ordered to remain in it and resist at all costs. According to Axworthy despite this, the situation inside the pocket was quite complicated, as they lacked food and only had about 40 shots per man. A column with fuel reached the Romanian positions and at dawn on the next day, Junkers Ju-52 of the 105th German Transport Squadron managed to supply some of the materials they needed; despite both contributions of fuel, this was never in enough quantities. The Soviets tried to surrender the pocket to avoid further losses, but they found the refusal of Major General Lascar who also tried to break the pocket during the night of the 22nd. The 15th Infantry Division was chosen to start this attack in the southwest direction (towards Bol.Donschynka) while the 6th Infantry Division headed towards Petshany. During the combats, Lascar was taken prisoner, leaving Major General Sion in charge of the escape attempt. Despite the Romanian attempts to escape, the Soviets managed to overtake them and practically annihilate the Romanian unit.

The Romanian troops that managed to escape and reach Bol.Donschynka joined the 22nd Panzer Division and the 1st Romanian Armored Division. These surviving troops of the "General Lascar" Combat Group were ordered to defend the town of Chernashevskaya.

During the withdrawal to the south, the arrival of the remains of the 1st Tank Regiment commanded by Romanian Captain Arcadie Duceac, allowed the 22nd Panzer Division to retreat thanks to the fact that they managed to stop the enemy advance for about eight hours, leaving the Romanians as rearguard and again helpless before the fierce Soviet attacks.

Returning again to the actions of the Romanian 1st Armored Division, we are at dawn on November 24; in fact at 5.00 am. At that time a new Soviet armored attack unleashed a powerful strike over the units in front of them. In this case a Mechanized Group located north of Riabuhin and remains of the 3rd Motorized Vanatori Regiment in Oserski. The poor situation of the Romanian troops, exhausted and with shortage of supplies motivated that the Soviets fought against little Romanian resistance. This fact was demonstrated in the fighting for Chernashevskaya, since the Romanians who defended this town lacked anti-tank parts, artillery and of course German support tanks. Again, the few battle tanks in combat conditions belonging to the 1st Romanian Armored Division 1st Tank Regiment had to delay the advance of the Soviets without any support of their own infantry or artillery with limited counterattacks like the one that happened on November 26. That same day starting from their positions located about 3 kilometers south of Chernashevskaya, Romanian tanks attacked Soviet positions to the north and northeast of Chernashevskaya.

The same afternoon of the 24th the Romanian survivors of this new Soviet attack (among which were the battered remnants of the 1st Romanian Armored Division) managed to break the contact with the Soviet cavalry troops that harassed them and marched after the 22nd Panzer Division in the direction of the Chir River (which represented the first defensive line of the Axis capable of stopping the Soviet advance). After a week of continuous clashes with the Soviets during their withdrawal, the Romanian vanguard units managed to reach the Chir River on November 25 and cross it, to become part of the defensive line that the Axis was preparing to stop the Soviet onslaught. Being more accurate, they finally reached in the vicinity of Chernashevskaya at 02:00 on the 25th to cross the river Chir by the bridge in Gussinka shortly after. A very important fact to remember is that if the Romanian units were very battered, the Germans were not better; in fact the almost complete lack of fuel of the vehicles of the 22nd Panzer Division, motivated that finally the Romanians after contacting their German comrades should even give part of their fuel to them. But while the vanguard of the Romanian 1st Armored Division tried to reorganize itself once crossed the river, the Romanian rearguard had not yet crossed and it would maintain diverse confrontations with the Soviets, like the one that took place on the south of the Chernashevskaya locality during the attack at the 302 hill. Despite the disastrous Romanian retreat, they were able to improve their defensive lines in the Chir, thanks to the fact that the Soviets also had to pause to properly reorganize and consolidate their positions in the Solotovski and Mikhailska area.

After the protection of the Chir River defensive line, the remains of the 1st Romanian Armored Division (only 5 tanks R-2 and 1 T-3 in operation had managed to reach the "security" of crossing the Chir River, having lost the rest of armored in the previous days), they occupied their positions in the defensive framework. The withdrawal of the Romanians caused a loss of more than 80% of their troops to reach new positions about 25-30 kilometers south of the Chir River.

Between November 27 and December 1, the 1st Armored Division tried to keep the Soviet troops in their positions by attacking small bridgeheads that the Soviets had on the Chir River. In these small clashes, the Division suffered about 500 casualties, including dead, frozen and wounded.

On December 2 the Romanian 1st Armored Division had two tanks in service and about 944 men of the initial 12,000; so it can practically be considered that its usefulness at the front was zero. The limited number of men and vehicles in combat conditions determined that a reorganization of the units of the Division was carried out in the so-called Detasamentul colonel Nistor or "Colonel Nistor" Detachment commanded by Colonel Nistor. So on December 4 they were incorporated into the so-called "Colonel Nistor" Detachment. The two armored vehicles that were still in service at that time were joined by four more tanks after being repaired (without being able to specify the type), some German armored vehicles and half-tracks (again according to Axworthy on December 12, 10 SdKfz 222 and on December 19 8 SdKfz 251 were received); also, a short time later around 700 men and 1 R-2 from the Armored Division deposit in Romania joined. Despite this and due to the bad shape, the remains of the 1st Armored Division were ordered to support the 3rd Motorized Regiment (Vanatori) on the Chir River front.

They would remain in their new defensive positions until the afternoon of December 23, when the High Command ordered the withdrawal of the Romanian troops to form a defensive line in the heights north of Glinaja (in the area of Solotovski and Mihailovka, where the Soviets were also in a period of reorganization).

In the successive combats that took place on the night between December 25 and 26 in the vicinity of Solotovsky, the few tanks that were still in service in the 1st Tank Regiment commanded by Captain Arcadie Duceac along with the 3rd Motorized Vanatori Regiment 1st Battalion counterattacked the Soviet vanguards belonging to the 22nd Guards Motorized Brigade that tried to penetrate in the northwest area of the village, in the sector where the men belonging to the Mechanized Group and from the 3rd Motorized Vanatori Regiment were placed. Thanks to the Romanian reaction, the enemy attack was stopped, causing numerous casualties. The fights inside the town lasted until 5.20 pm, when the Romanian troops were finally authorized to retreat to less exposed positions in Gurin-Bistrij (about 15 km east of the town of Moroszovskaja). This was another example of the innumerable attacks and counterattacks that took place during the painful withdrawal of the Romanian troops in these days of December. In these combats, the captain Duceac was able to return to his lines despite having been seriously damaged his tank. Thanks to the valiant actions of the last days of December, Captain Duceac was granted several decorations.

The "Colonel Nistor" Detachment had fulfilled the mission entrusted to them within its deployment in the defense of the Chir River to prevent the crossing of it by the Soviets; however, in those clashes against the 22nd Guards Motorized Brigade, "Colonel Nistor" Detachment would definitely lose the few armored vehicles they had (on December 24, 3 Romanian tanks were lost, and on December 26 another 2 Romanian tanks were lost in exchange for destroying 2 tanks and 2 Soviet armored vehicles).

The Romanian 1st Armored Division, despite the adverse circumstances they had to face, maintained continuous confrontations against the Soviets for several days trying to quell the danger of the cut by the Soviets of the only escape of the German-Romanian troops towards the River Chir. They had managed to escape the powerful Soviet advance and reach the "relative" security offered by the River Chir at first, and then avoid as far as possible the collapse of the German-Romanian defensive system in the Chir and the subsequent withdrawal.

The courageous behavior demonstrated by the men of the Romanian 1st Armored Division during their retreat and especially in the defensive fighting in the

Chir River caused them to be mentioned in the Order of the Day n° 14 of October 12, 1943 in the following way: "The towns of Oserski, Osinovski, Solotovski and Chernashevskaya are the main places where the Romanian 1st Armored Division shed its blood and took its place in the most impressive page in history that the Romanian armies wrote in the steppes of the Don." Despite the large number of casualties suffered and although some Romanian troops withdrew before the Soviet avalanche, in general the Romanian troops had fought without ceasing and managed to slow the advance of the Soviets towards the Chir River.

The 83,000 men of the 3rd Romanian Army, who managed to escape the Soviets, would now be part of the "Hollidt" Army Detachment which had remnants of the 7th, 9th and 11th Infantry Divisions, 7th Cavalry Division and the 1st Armored Division; as well as the 22nd Panzer Division, which were arranged along the Chir River.

It is necessary to remember that towards the end of November of 1942 the operation Wintergewitter (Winter Storm) was created that would consist in an attack by the Don Army Group in the Chir River Front in order to try to arrive at Stalingrad in order to break the Soviet siege in the city. This operation that would count with the 57th Panzer Corps, the 48th Panzer Corps and the "Hollidt" Army Detachment, was not successful.

On December 11, 1942, the 16th and 3rd Soviet Guard Armies, the operation "Little Saturn" (whose objective would be to cross the Don and reach Rostov) began against the troops of the 8th Italian Army, marginally positioned the "Hollidt" Army Detachment which was deployed along the river Chir and where the Romanians of the 3rd Army were assigned as we have said.

Although it leaves our subject of study, with respect to the Romanian 4th Army (remember that it was subordinated to the IV Panzer Army in the sector of Stalingrad under constant Soviet pressure), we must say that on November 20 it received the Soviet attack from the 51st and 57th Armies that completely broke the Romanian defensive line; causing that diverse Romanian units were surrounded before the impetus of the Soviet advance. On the 23rd, the 4th Army HQ after the great strike received by the Soviets and the desperate situation that created in the Romanian troops requested the IV Panzer Army permission to act independently of them; he received that permission from the German high command. In any case, the situation was very complicated due to the attack of many Soviet armored units.

A column of Soviet tanks T-34/85 progress through the Eastern Front during 1943-1944. These tanks with its mighty gun were some tough rivals for the Romanian armored forces.
[From public domain]

Two Romanian pilots pose in front of a Bf.109 E in 1943. You can see the great Michael Cross in the fuselage of the plane. This badge was similar to that used by the armored forces for their recognition from the air. The Romanian aviation lent its aid to its compatriots during the different phases of the war. [Courtesy by George from Historice.ro]

A Romanian anti-tank gun in action during the fighting in Crimea. The 50 T-38 supplied by Germany to Romania slightly alleviated the large deficit in anti-tank weapons of the Romanian troops. [Courtesy by George from Historice.ro]

The weather conditions in which the Romanian soldiers met during the winter in the USSR were very hard, as can be seen in this photograph taken in 1943. [Courtesy by George from Historice.ro]

Various Romanian T-38 (Pz.Kpfw.38 (t) according to the German name) in Crimea during 1943, where they were integrated into the so-called Batalionul care da lupta T-38 that was divided into three Companies: 51st Company, 52nd Company and 53rd Company. Although they were obsolete tanks when Romania received them, the T-38 represented an improvement over the R-2 or R-35. [Courtesy by George from Historice.ro]

Two Romanian gunners prepare to fire their 47mm Bohler anti-tank gun. Among the main needs of the Romanian armored forces were the anti-tank guns. [Courtesy by Pusca and Nitu from worldwar2.ro from MMN]

Given the shortage of anti-tank guns in Romania, Germany was responsible for providing various models. This photo shows several gunners firing a 50 mm Pak 38 in Kuban in 1943. [Courtesy by Pusca and Nitu from worldwar2.ro and Armata Romana 1941-1945]

The most powerful tank that Romania had during WWII was the T-4 (the German Pz.Kpfw. IV in different models such as the F2, G, H or J) thanks to its long 75mm cannon. The picture shows a T-4 (possibly a G model) in the parade that took place on May 10, 1943, months after the Stalingrad disaster. [Courtesy by Pusca and Nitu from worldwar2.ro]

Several gunners firing a 75 mm Vickers Resita gun in the USSR in May 1943. [Courtesy by Pusca and Nitu from worldwar2.ro and Armata Romana 1941-1945]

The Cavalry Units had an anti-tank Cavalry Company equipped with small-caliber anti-tank guns. In the photograph we see the crew of a small Bofors anti-tank gun used by cavalry troops in May 1943. [Courtesy by Pusca and Nitu from worldwar2.ro]

One of the "cargo mules" of the Romanian mechanized forces, the Famo halftracked carrier. These vehicles were completely necessary to provide mobility to the Romanian canyons. In the photograph we see a Famo preserved in the National Military Museum of Bucharest. [Courtesy by Pusca and Nitu from worldwar2.ro]

Photograph of an R-35 at the National Military Museum in Bucharest. Although at first they were considered suitable tanks for combat, later they had to be relegated to secondary tasks and training. Several R-35s were modernized by replacing their original cannon with a 45mm one, giving rise to the so-called Vanatorul de care R-35. [Picture by Dragos Pusca and courtesy by Pusca and Nitu from worldwar2.ro]

Photograph of the same R-35 at the National Military Museum in Bucharest where you can see the shield of the Michael Cross on the back hull of the tank. The thick armor that he had made him very appreciated in the fight against the trenches in Odessa. [Picture by Dragos Pusca and courtesy by Pusca and Nitu from worldwar2.ro]

Two images showing several soldiers during their anti-tank instruction. The "enemy" tank is on this occasion a T-38. The lack of an adequate number of anti-tank weapons in Romania resulted in the use of soldiers directly in the anti-tank fight. [Courtesy by Pusca and Nitu from worldwar2.ro]

Antitank gun 75mm DT-UDR 26 Model 1943 Reșița. This gun with similar characteristics to the German PaK 40 would have increased the anti-tank Romanian power of having been manufactured in greater quantities. [From public domain - by Mircea87]

German Pz.Kpfw. V "Panther" in 1944 on the Romanian Front. The "Grossdeutschland" Division managed to keep the Romanian front line during the spring of 1944 despite multiple Soviet attacks. [From Bundesarchiv, Bild 101I-244-2321-34 Waidelich CC-BY-SA 3.0A]

A column of German "Panther" tanks belonging to the "Grossdeutschland" Division advancing along a road in poor condition on the Romanian Front in April 1944. [From Bundesarchiv, Bild 183-J24359 CC-BY-SA 3.0]

Several Romanian soldiers traveling in an SPW in the Transylvanian Front after the change of side of Romania in August 1944. [From Internet - From Online communism photo collection 41962X60X96 (27.03.2018) elevation 1671944 photo # MA058]

Soviet troops cheered on the streets of Bucharest on August 31, 1944. Although in principle many Rumanians saw the liberation of the control that Germany exercised over Romania very positive, they would soon realize that history would repeat itself but now under the control of the USSR. [From public domain]

A TACAM T-60 is studied in Kubinka during the trials to which it was subjected after its capture. This tank destroyer was completely obsolete compared to the armored vehicles available to the Red Army. [Courtesy of tankarchives]

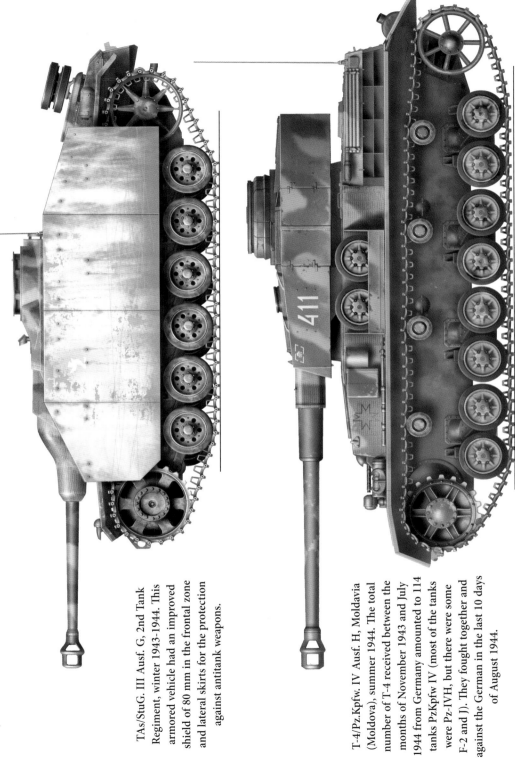

Painted by Arkadiusz Wróbel

TAs/StuG. III Ausf. G, 2nd Tank Regiment, winter 1943-1944. This armored vehicle had an improved shield of 80 mm in the frontal zone and lateral skirts for the protection against antitank weapons.

T-4/Pz.Kpfw. IV Ausf. H, Moldavia (Moldova), summer 1944. The total number of T-4 received between the months of November 1943 and July 1944 from Germany amounted to 114 tanks PzKpfw IV (most of the tanks were Pz-IVH, but there were some F-2 and J). They fought together and against the German in the last 10 days of August 1944.

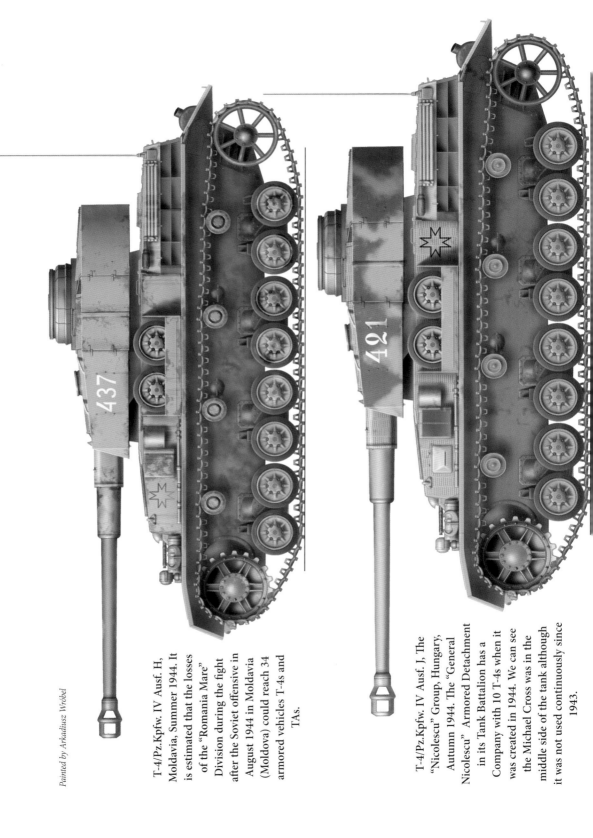

Painted by Arkadiusz Wróbel

T-4/Pz.Kpfw. IV Ausf. H, Moldavia, Summer 1944. It is estimated that the losses of the "Romania Mare" Division during the fight after the Soviet offensive in August 1944 in Moldavia (Moldova) could reach 34 armored vehicles T-4s and TAs.

T-4/Pz.Kpfw. IV Ausf. J, The "Nicolescu" Group, Hungary, Autumn 1944. The "General Nicolescu" Armored Detachment in its Tank Battalion has a Company with 10 T-4s when it was created in 1944. We can see the Michael Cross was in the middle side of the tank although it was not used continuously since 1943.

CHAPTER VII

1943. Reorganization After The Disaster

Again following the works of Nitu, Pusca, Axworthy, Cloutier, Zaloga and Filipescu, we will explain the reconstruction of the Romanian Armored Forces after the first two years of war.

The Romanian Army lost 158854 men wounded, dead and missing during the Stalingrad campaign from November 19, 1942 to January 7, 1943, which represented almost half of the Romanian Army. The Romanian 1st Armored Division suffered a very high number of casualties in both men and vehicles: according to most of the consulted sources 86 tanks (around 1/3 were destroyed by the Soviets, but most of them had to be left behind due to breakdown or lack of fuel mainly) and 678 vehicles of all types were lost, in addition to 130 officers, 87 non-commissioned officers, 3067 soldiers and at least 3000 men with varying degrees of freezing (in addition to the important human losses, it is necessary to emphasize that they were the most prepared and trained in Romania for the handling of armored vehicles, reason why only in several battle days, great part of these veterans and of the experienced crews disappeared of the Romanian Army with the consequences that this would bring in the immediate future of the country). Also 474 rifles, 22 guns, 55 mortars, 129 light machine guns and 22 heavy machine guns were lost in the 1st Romanian Armored Division so it practically was no longer operative (they only kept in service about 40 R- 2 in bad conditions, which were mostly those that had been stored in deposits when arriving at the Chir river and never got to deploy in combat). In fact, both the Romanian Armored forces and the Romanian Army in general, would never fully recover from the Stalingrad disaster. As a curiosity, the R-1 tanks were practically lost in combat, so that in some units of the Romanian Cavalry, some Stuart tanks captured from the Soviets had to be used punctually. Among all lost R-2, almost two thirds were due to varied breakdown and only one third due to enemy fire. On the other hand the air branch of the Romanian army also suffered important losses in those days; 76 aircraft of the Romanian Air Corps were lost, of which 26 were shot down and the others destroyed on the ground.

On February 2, 1943, the resistance in Stalingrad by the Axis forces ceased. Of the 91,000 prisoners made in the city, only 3,000 were Romanians, belonging to the remains of the 20th Infantry Division, 1st Cavalry Division and the "Colonel Voicu" Detachment.

The disaster that occurred in Stalingrad not only brought with it the practical annihilation of thousands and thousands of Axis soldiers, but also caused a great problem in the German defensive structure in the southern area of the USSR. The lines of communication in the southern area of Ukraine controlled by the Axis were in imminent danger of being attacked by the avalanche of Soviet troops. The German and Romanian troops had to take new positions to make more effective the Axis defense lines. So the 2nd Mountain Division (Vanatori) marched towards Rostov, and the 17th Army was sent to the Taman peninsula. It would be in this area, where fierce fighting would take place between February and September 1943 in Kuban. For their part, the Soviets tried to isolate all possible Romanian-German troops within the Crimean peninsula; as it happened with those that were besieged in the area of Sevastopol until May 1944. Many of these besieged troops managed to return behind their own lines thanks to the maritime evacuation that was carried out by the Romanian Navy in the so-called "Operation 60000". This Operation was carried out in two phases, the first between April 12 and May 5, 1944; and the second between May 6 and May 13, 1944, obtaining a number of German evacuees of 58486, of whom 12027 were injured; and of the Romanians of 36557, of whom 4262 were injured (a few hundred Slovaks and a few thousand Russian volunteers who served the German Reich were also evacuated).

Reconstruction Of The Romanian Armored Forces

Returning to the Romanian armored troops, like the other Romanian troops that managed to escape the disaster of Stalingrad, they were sent back to the fatherland. The tanks that were in the process of repair at the beginning of the year 1943 were 54 F-17, 2 T-4, 2 T-3, 25 R-2 and 52 R-35. The degree of destruction of the Romanian Armored Division was such that it was in the process of reconstruction relegated to training tasks, and would not be operational until August 1944, changing its commander in chief who became Major General Nicolae Stoenescu from the March 21, 1943. During that year and a half, it was achieved, at least partially, to rebuild the structure of the Division thanks to the fundamental help of the German industry. In fact, practically all the armored vehicles that were in the combat front after the Soviet attack to Stalingrad were lost, being able to save only the vehicles that were in repair period in factories when the combats happened in the Romanian hinterland.

The critical situation of the Romanian armored weapon motivated that proposals to improve it began to appear, such as the one contributed by Col. Guilai, who in January 1943 suggested the incorporation of a 45 mm cannon (of those captured by the Soviets) in replacement of the original barrel in the R-35. Everything that could be done to increase the caliber of the Romanian armor was of great help in the recomposition of the Romanian armored forces. This project would be released as late as June 1944 with only 30 copies called Vanatorul of Care R-35 Transformat.

In the face of such a situation, the Romanian General Staff agreed that it was necessary to order supplies of battle tanks from their German ally. These cars should be at the same skill of their Soviet enemies and should be supplied in adequate quantities (taking into account the practical destruction of the Armored Division, it would be an important number of tanks). During 1943, the 1st Armored Division was re-equipped and the 5th and 8th cavalry divisions were fully motorized and then the idea was to convert them into armored divisions. But the German response could not be more disappointing for the Romanians, since the only material that was sent to them as stipulated in the Birnbaum Program, were 50 Pz.kpfw.38 (t) from the Ausf.A, B and C models (tanks of Czechoslovak origin originally called ČKD LT VZ 38). These tanks had been used by the Germans and after they had been subjected to an incomplete set-up that would have to be finished by the Romanians themselves. In Romania they received the name of T-38, that had the same name that a Soviet amphibious tank, of which the Rumanians had captured some units. Despite this, the two types of tanks maintained the name of T-38.

According to Axworthy, on July 15, 1943 the 1st Armored Division that should have 2767 vehicles had a large part of them under repair (as it happened to the 5th and 8th Cavalry Divisions). In fact, the complete motorization of the 8th Cavalry Division was delayed until the summer of 1944 (and only thanks to borrowing vehicles from the 5th Cavalry Division, which never was fully motorized).

The reason for the scarce German aid has to be assessed according to the attitude of Germany up to that moment with its allies. To begin the need for armored material for the German Army itself was continuous due to its wear in the different combat fronts where Germany had troops fighting. In fact, the German Army used without any doubt captured battle tanks to various enemies against whom they had fought, as is the case of Czechoslovakia, France, the USSR or the United Kingdom. For this reason, it turned out that Germany was quite reluctant to supply any type of armored material to its allies and especially first level material (which was exclusively reserved for use by German troops). Despite this, we must remember that although in very low numbers, the Romanians also used some T-60 and even some T-34, as well as other armored vehicles such as the German half-track "Famo" (from which a large number were delivered from Germany between 1939 and 1944), Tatra vz. 29, Škoda vz.27, Škoda vz.25, Autoblinda 41, BA-10 or BA-64.

Therefore, the 50 obsolete T-38 that Germany supplied to Romania can be considered as a drop in the sea. There were few tanks (taking into account the annihilation of the armored forces between December 1942 and January 1943), very outdated and deteriorated by previous use, with little armor and inadequate armament. In addition Germany only agreed to supply these tanks with one condition: they could only be used in the frontline and never in the rearguard or in Romania itself; in fact they should be sent to the Romanians directly to the Kuban bridgehead operational area.

As we can see, despite the very low utility of the Pz.kpfw.38 (t) tanks from Czech origin, Romania could not help but feel grateful to the powerful German Reich for having attended to their requests, at least in part. Apart from the T-38 the only major increase in the armored force in 1943 were 34 TACAM T-60 (for the 61st and 62nd TACAM Companies), and 30 Komsomolyets artillery tractors that were repaired.

It was finally in March 1943 when the 50 T-38s were handed out to the Romanians. These tanks were first sent to the Crimea, where in June 1943 the Romanian crews were trained in their new tanks. The 50 tanks were intended to reinforce the Romanian Cavalry Corps and Mountain Corps; for which an Armored Battalion (Batalionul care da lupta T-38) was constituted that was divided into 3 Companies with 15 tanks each: 51st Company, 52nd Company and 53rd Company. The remaining five tanks were kept in reserve to cover the possible losses of the three companies although according to some source they acted as command unit (or 54th Company).

Also in March 1943 but in this case in Romania itself the so-called Rapid Detachment was formed with the surviving remains of the 1st Armored Division (according to Axworthy, it was formed in August). With this Detachment it was intended to lay the basis for a new armored unit and therefore to serve as a training unit. The supply of vehicles belonged to a Company of self-propelled guns with 12 TACAM T-60, 1 Antiaircraft and 1 Antitank Company, 1 Motorized Artillery Battalion and 1 Liaison Vehicle (1 Sdkfz 222).

Returning to Crimea, the arrival of the T-38 was an initial joy for the Romanians followed by a great disappointment since only 17 of them were in operational status to be received by the Romanian troops. This fact motivated that the Romanian maintenance services and the own crews that have to handle T-38s would have to work many hours to finally put them all in service. Finally, after overcoming these initial problems, the T-38 were sent to the place where the Germans had agreed with the Romanians, in which they were to be deployed: at Kuban bridgehead. Recall that one of the requirements imposed on the Romanians by the Germans to give them these tanks was to use them on the front line exclusively.

The arrival of the T-38s to Kuban really contributed little to the balance of the opposing forces there. In fact, in a few days 7 T-38s were out of service due to the actions of the Soviet antitank and infantry. Inevitably, the German-Romanian defenses in Taman were yielding to the Soviet power, fighting in the Perekop peninsula and had to retreat towards Crimea. There, what remained operative of the Batalionul care da lupta T-38 would participate in the clashes in retreat during the last part of the year 1943 (it is estimated that from the 50 initial T-38s, some 16 were lost in combat, and at least 19 were abandoned).

On July 28, the 51st and 52nd Companies were transferred to the Kuban bridgehead, being subordinated to the Cavalry Corps.

On September 10, the Soviets launched an offensive aimed to destroy the Romanian-German bridgehead in Kuban. Given this situation, the withdrawal of the Axis troops towards Crimea began. In this context the Romanian T-38 began to fight in the clashes that took place the first days of November 1943, since on November 1 the 4th Ukrainian Front began its offensive on Crimea, succeeding in establishing a bridgehead south of the Sivash Sea. Precisely that area was defended by various Romanian units: the 15th, 23rd and 24th Mountain Battalions, the 4th Artillery Regiment 2nd Battalion, the 37th Antitank Company and the 53rd Armored Company. All these units were framed in the 1st and 2nd Romanian Mountain Divisions. The 53rd Armored Company was integrated into the 2nd Mountain Division under the command of Colonel Grigore Balan.

Before the Soviet attack, the 53rd Armored Company was called urgently, reaching Karanky on the night of November 3 to 4, to attack with his 12 T-38 available against Soviet positions only one day after (the 5th) under the command of Captain Ioan Cernea. This courageous attack drove the Soviets back, allowing the Romanians to advance northwards by about 9 kilometers. During the violent fighting sustained, the chief of the Company, Cernea, was killed.

Also the 51st and 52nd Armored Companies participated in trying to prevent the Soviet landing in the Crimea, but the thin armor of Romanian tanks was too vulnerable to 45mm anti-tank guns and Soviet anti-tank rifles.

The wear suffered by the Romanian armored troops was very high, so that for example, the 53rd Armored Company at the end of November had only 3 operational T-38 tanks.

The Soviet advance in Crimea was unstoppable for the Germans and Romanians (although the Germans were who mostly supported the defensive effort). The Romanian 10th Division defended the eastern flank of the retreating Axis troops in the area of the Isthmus of Perekop. Between November 1 and 6, the Soviets established a bridgehead in Sivash. According to Axworthy, the Romanian troops still had the support of 12 T-38 that belonged to the 53rd Armored Company; although 2 T-38 were destroyed on November 4 in a Romanian counterattack in Karanki and 4 T-38 were lost in the later clashes for Kriatskoe.

Between November 2, 1943 and January 21, 1944, the 54th Armored Company (initially used as an HQ and training unit) supported the actions of the Romanian Mountain Corps. The 54th Armored Company had the initial 5 T-38s to which 3 T-38s from the 53rd Armored Company were added.

Between November 1 and 10, the 3rd Romanian Mountain Division supported by T-38 of the 51st and 52nd Armored Companies repelled some landing attempts on the Kerch peninsula.

On November 30, 15 T-38 of the 51st Armored Company were repatriated to Romania. On December 12, 5 T-38 from the 52nd Company were sent to Romania. In December, the T-38 that remained operative to Batalionul care da lupta T-38 were only 10, which finally would be sent to Romania at the beginning of 1944 (some source still places 10 T-38 belonging to the 53rd Company in Crimea in April of 1944 in support missions to the 10th Infantry Division).

According to Axworthy, and returning to the 1st Armored Division, this unit on April 1, 1943 had 59 R-2 (but only 16 in service), while the 2nd Armored Regiment still had 52 R-35s, a T-3 and a T-4, on February 4, 1943; 8 R-35s were in training centers. In the

Cavalry Training Center there were 14 R-1; so there were 62 FT-17 available in Romania. On April 15, 207 tanks owned by Romanians, 203 can be considered as completely obsolete for use in combat. On August 30, the tanks were distributed as follows:

- 1st Armored Regiment: 55 R-2 (30 in repair).

- 2nd Regiment of tanks: 52 R-35 (6 in repair), 62 FT-17 (8 in repair), 1 T-3 and 1 T-4.

- Cavalry and training units: 13 R-1 (8 under repair), 8 R-35 (possibly 3 under repair), 13 FT-17 and possibly 4 R-2 under repair.

During 1943-1944 Antonescu increased his personal guard regiment to 3 battalions, counting the 2nd battalion with 6 FT-17 tanks platoon. Although completely outdated for their use in combat, they were suitable for police and surveillance tasks.

As last information of the Romanian armored forces in the year of 1943, we have the fact that in October of 1943 the Romanian High Command decided to dissolve the Rapid Detachment that served as a training unit for a future Romanian armored unit. This fact was motivated because on October 28 the guidelines to be followed for the creation of a Command of Mechanized troops, the 1st Armored Training Division and the 8th Motorized Regiment were promulgated. Romania was preparing to have again armored and motorized forces after the disaster of the end of 1942, and requested new material from Germany. Meanwhile, as happened in Hungary, Romania tried unsuccessfully to create an industrial infrastructure that would allow it to manufacture its own armored vehicles; whose designs as we will see were promising. So the national project based on the chassis of the T-60 with the 76.2 mm F22 cannon began to come true, since in June 1943 17 Tun self-propelled cu afet mobil T-60 (better known by the name TACAM T -60) left the production lines. These vehicles would be used for the reconstruction of the 1st Armored Division, in full process at that time. Also the Romanian industry developed the production of its hybrid vehicles with the R-35/45 (30 R-35 were improved in its barrel with a new 45mm canon then to be called R-35/45). But both these conversions from R-35 to R-35/45 and from TACAM R-2 would not come true until August 1944.

In the autumn of 1943, Romanians finally managed to get one of their requests for new non-obsolete armored material accepted by Germany. Following the guidelines of the Olivenbaum Program (on September 23, 1943 the Germans agreed to carry out the armored delivery program called Olivenbaum I, which should be followed by the II and III), they proceeded to the sale of armored material between the months of November 1943 and July 1944. With the new armored vehicles that Germany sent to Romania they were trying to achieve the transformation of the 1st Armored Division into a unit able to fight in the same skill conditions in front of the Soviet armored units. The vehicles that were sold were 114 tanks Pz.Kpfw IV (most of the tanks were Pz.IVH, but there were some F-2 and J), 98 StuG III (assault guns), and 2 BefPz.Wg IV (command vehicles based on Pz. IV, of which 3 copies had been promised). In addition, 40 Sdkfz 222, 8 Italian armored vehicles and 27 armored half-tracks were promised. However, most of them were in very poor maintenance conditions.

CHAPTER VIII

1944. Between The Sword And The Wall

At the beginning of the year, the Romanian 1st Armored Division returned to the "security" of its homeland by its own means at the end of March. From this moment resumed its period of rebuilding with the arrival of the new armored vehicles from Germany after having been practically annihilated in the front of Stalingrad. The Romanian High Command therefore had time to assess the behavior and results of its armored forces after their confrontation with the Soviets. The conclusions were several:

- The training received by the men of the armored units was almost never adequate. In fact, the tanks were used almost exclusively as support for the Romanian land units, without ever making a joint use of them. In addition, the training of the crews was not standardized, so there were units better prepared than others, without a specific justification. This lack of adequate training was appreciated in the campaigns of Stalingrad and Crimea, where what really enabled the operation of the armored troops was the courage of their men. With the progress of the war, there were many raiders who died or were injured and unfit to return to their units, so these men who were more prepared for combat could not be used as the basis of a better prepared armored force. Only the few surviving tank crews of the Stalingrad and Crimean campaigns became the elite of the Romanian armored forces and therefore they were the ones that received the best vehicles in the improved 1st Armored Division in 1944.

- Another factor that had a negative influence was the fact of owning quite obsolete tanks when Romania began its intervention in the armed conflict. This motivated that better results were never achieved, unlike what the Germans did. It is true that the armored material that Romania had did not come close to the quality of the German material, but this obsolescence, together with the wrong tactics when using the armored ones, completely hampered its proper use in combat.

The arrival of modern material of German origin as the Pz. III and Pz. IV at the end of 1942, was a significant improvement within the 1st Romanian Armored Division, but the attack carried out by the Soviets practically did not make it possible for the crews to get a suitable dominion of the new armored material. In addition, the continuous withdrawal in which the Axis troops were immersed in those days did not allow the Pz. III and Pz. IV (T-3 and T-4) to be used more than in small counterattacks or fighting withdrawal.

Finally, it will be in 1944 when new armored vehicles of German origin were incorporated into the Romanian Division such as StuG III Ausf.G (TA for Romanians) and more modern models of Pz. IV (type H); but in this case in an abundant number, so that could finally create a Romanian armored unit able to fight as equal to the Soviet units. We will see, as it did not get the right performance to these modern armored vehicles due again to the wrong tactics followed by the Romanian armored troops.

The anti-tank capability of the Romanian tanks had to be complemented by the anti-tank guns, so that only when the 75 mm Pak 40 and Reșița M43 guns arrived in adequate numbers during 1944, the Romanian Army acquired a significant anti-tank capability.

Despite German the aid in 1944, Romania was already defensive against a powerful Soviet advance, something which prevented the Romanian armored forces from recovering after the Stalingrad disaster.

- In relation to the previous factor, the almost absolute dependence by the Romanian part of Germany in terms of armored vehicles acted in a very negative way in the use of the Romanian armored troops. The German inability to self-supply with armored vehicles caused them to have to use vehicles captured by the enemy on several occasions (the so-called Panzerbeute), so the needs of armored vehicles of the allied countries passed into the background, always after Germany. This fact motivated that, especially between 1942 and 1943, the vehicles received from Germany in many cases had been used until exhaustion by the Germans, who after a few repairments and set-ups delivered them to their Romanian ally (this not only happened with Germany, but with the other allied countries of Germany).

- The last factor that had such a negative influence on Romanian armored forces was the country's inability to manufacture armored vehicles. Its Hungarian neighbor, in spite of the many difficulties they had during the world conflict, managed to build an indigenous industry of armored vehicles that gave rise to the Toldi and Touran cars, the Zrínyi assault cannon or the Csaba tanquette.

The National Industry To The Rescue

The attempts of the national industry to build national design tanks under German license was unsuccessful. Following the works of Nitu, Pusca, Axworthy, and Zaloga we know that the Romanian industrial incapacity, together with the destruction caused by the allied bombings, meant that only hybrids TACAM R-2 or T-60 vehicles could be manufactured in a modest number, and vehicles such as the excellent

Mareşal tank destroyer were not manufactured in series; causing Romania to lose the opportunity of self-sufficiency even if it was partially in terms of armored vehicles.

The history of the Mareşal deserves to be remembered, as Romania lost the opportunity to finally have a really first-class self-propelled gun. Already in the summer of 1943 a prototype of assault gun was built with the chassis of a T-60 and a 122 mm howitzer (also Soviet) obr. 04/30. The official name was Vanatorul de Care Mareşal. In spite of carrying a howitzer (as it happened with the Hungarian Zrínyi), the ammunition was modified so that it had an adequate anti-tank effect. The expectation with the prototype grew, but it was decided to change the weapon for a smaller caliber but with greater anti-tank potential; we refer to the Romanian-made 75 mm Reşiţa gun (the 4th prototype, completed in February 1944, already incorporating the 75 mm gun). The Mareşal armored vehicle then started on a T-60 chassis, although the development of the war and the dependency of Germany in terms of supplies caused the 5th and 6th prototypes to use more pieces from Pz.Kpfw 38 (t), which was still in production. The suitable qualities on anti-tank combat of the Mareşal were not underestimated by the Germans; in fact, according to some historians, the famous German Hetzer (made of the chassis of the Pz.Kpfw 38 (t)) was clearly inspired by the Romanian armor. In addition, even the German Reich considered the acquisition of the Romanian armor in an antiaircraft version (Flak Panzer) equipped with a 37 mm fast gun. But any further development of the Mareşal both in its anti-tank version and in its antiaircraft version were unsuccessful after the destruction of the Romanian industries, where it was manufactured due to bombings by US aircrafts. Perhaps if they had had some more time it would have been possible to resume the manufacturing of the Mareşal, but the arrival of the Soviets and the subsequent defection of Romania definitively ended with this promising armored car. We dedicate a small chapter to this vehicle in the annexes.

Concerning the TACAM R-2, it is necessary to remember the cause of the important delay that the execution of this program had (this project started simultaneously with the TACAM T-60, which had already been released in June 1943). The R-2 although obsolete was the main tank that the Romanians had after the disaster of Stalingrad, so the Romanian High Command did not want to start the conversion into a self-propelled car until all the T-38 were received from Germany. So, although the UMP and Leonida industries in Bucharest were ready to begin with the conversion, they could not start until as late as February 1944 (when the original plan was due to begin in August 1943). The first 20 converted R-2 left the production lines in July 1944 and were also the last since the program was canceled due to the course the conflict was taking, with the battlefront in Romanian borders. As we discussed earlier, the TACAM R-2 was to be equipped with the Soviet 76.2 mm Zis-3 cannon, but its shortage prompted the decision of the Romanian High Command to use the new 75 mm Reșița Romanian-made gun instead (which was a 76.2 mm Zis-3 with a caliber change to use the same ammunition of the German anti-tank gun PaK 40 of 75 mm) or with the famous 88 mm German cannon. As we know, the discontinuation of the conversion of this self-propelled gun made that this choice would not have any more relevance. The 20 specimens manufactured were all part of the same unit, the 63rd TACAM Company.

It was in June 1944 when 30 Vanatorul of Care R-35/45 Transformat were also received, based on the chassis of the R-35 with a turret mounting a Soviet 45 mm cannon. They were immediately sent to the 2nd Tank Regiment (where the R-35s that had been sent for modernization came from).

As a failed project of the Romanian industry it is necessary to remember the frustrated conversion of the obsolete R-1 into self-propelled guns equipped with a Soviet 45 mm cannon or the T-38 with Soviet 76.2 mm guns. Both programs never reached the production phase, but they do not leave any doubts about the Romanian's urgent need to increase the firepower of their armored vehicles.

Enemy On The Border

Again basing the text in Nitu, Pusca, Axworthy and Zaloga sources we know that before the Soviet progression on the Eastern Front stepped into Romanian lands, the emergency lights went on. Romanian armored formations were needed at the front, but the 1st Armored Division was still in full reorganization period. An emergency solution had to be found, which consisted on creating a partially armored unit, which could be sent to the front. So, on February 24, the so-called Grupului Mixt Care of Luptă or "Cantemir" Mixed Armored Group in Northern Transnitria was created. This unit was made up of vehicles from the 1st Armored Division and by new vehicles from Germany and was formed as follows:
- 2 tank companies of: 30 T-4 and 2 T-3.
- 1 assault gun company: with 10 TA.
- 2 self-propelled gun batteries: with 14 TACAM T-60.
- 1 R-35 tank company.
- 1 R-2 tank company.

The "Cantemir" Mixed Armored Group was no more than an ephemeral unit that was created quickly and that lasted on the front until the end of March or the first of April (integrated in the III Corps in Transnistria), when it would eventually be integrated into the improved 1st Armored division. There was where the obsolete R-35 were used as stationary artillery due to its limited mobility. After that, the R-2 and R-35 still in service status were finally removed (on March 28, the R-35 and R-2 of the "Cantemir" Mixed Armored Group were removed and transferred to the town of Roman). While it was deployed in the front, another unit was being created in

Romania, called the Rapid Armored Detachment. This other unit was also supplied with vehicles belonging to the 1st Armored Division, and consisted of:

- 1 Tank Battalion: with two tank companies with 16 T-4 each one and a company of assault guns with 12 TA.
- 1 Vanatori motorized battalion.
- 1 motorized artillery battalion (with 12 Škoda 100 mm howitzers).
- 1 motorized anti-tank battalion: with 6 75 mm Reşiţa model 1943 anti-tank guns.
- 1 TACAM T-60 Battery.
- 1 anti-aircraft company.
- Medical Units and mixed services.

According to Axworthy the Rapid Armored Detachment was constituted as the embryo from which the 1st Armored Division was formed. Finally, the Rapid Armored Detachment was constituted by:

- 1st Armored Regiment 1st Battalion (16 T-4 and 12 TA).
- 1 Battalion of the 1st Motorized Artillery Regiment.
- 1 Battalion of the 3rd Motorized Rifle Regiment.
- 1 anti-tank battalion composed of 2 batteries: a battery with 7 TACAM T-60 and a battery with 6 guns of 75 mm PaK 97/38.
- A Reconnaissance Group made up of four Companies.

The advance of the Soviets during 1944 was constantly maintained on all fronts. With regard to the southern area of the USSR, on March 8 they entered through northern Ukraine and reached northern Bucovina on March 24 (taking over their capital Cernauti on March 29). This situation, with the Red Army so close, motivated that the 4th Romanian Army was activated to go towards the front, where it would meet the 3rd Army that was previously deployed. On March 16, Antonescu proposed to the Germans that the 3rd and 4th Armies could get together in the same Romanian Army Group, but this proposal was rejected by Hitler (at this point of the conflict, the German confidence in the Romanian ally was not much, for what they were not willing to allow a big Romanian unit exclusively under Romanian control).

The critical situation determined that the previously mentioned Rapid Armored Detachment was created on March 28 1944, which became the strongest armored unit in Romania, from which the Romanian 1st Armored Division would be rebuilt (we remember it because it had stood out in the front to the "Cantemir" Mixed Armored Group). In some cases, and always according to some sources, part of these vehicles was handled by German personnel in the absence of Romanian crews trained for it.

It was not long before the Rapid Armored Detachment was sent to the front, since at the end of March it was sent to Moldova. At the beginning of April 1944, the Soviet steamroller continued its advance capturing Odessa on April 10 and managing to take several bridgeheads along the Dniester River before slowing its advance. It was in the Moldovan front where the 1st Armored Division finally went back and on April 28 1944 it was named Romania Mare or Great Romania (the 26th according to Axworthy) as a resemblance of the German Grossdeutschland Division. The Division was under the command of Brigadier General Radu Korne from April 5 (according to Axworthy it was on the 7th, and his command lasted until the Division was dissolved in September 1944). On April 22 1944 the Division General Staff took command of the Rapid Armored Detachment near Roman.

Between March and April 1944, the city of Odessa returned to Soviet hands, so that the Soviets started the offensive that should end in the Balkans. The Soviets, despite coming dangerously close to Romania, were responsible for transmitting by radio that they had no territorial interests over Romania (evidently without including Bessarabia, which they considered part of their national territory); all focused on achieving a rapprochement of the Romanians to end with the change of side of Romania. On April 5, the bombing by the USAAF began on the Ploieşti oil fields and over the river traffic along the Danube river, which in just over a month and a half led to a reduction in Romanian oil production and its distribution in a very important way.

Since 1943 relations between Romania and Germany had clearly worsened, but the approach of the Soviets to Romanian lands definitely worsened them. This fact did not go unnoticed by Germany, who since the end of 1943 had had a special distrust of Romania, which was already beginning to show signs of its will to abandon the war. The German Reich chose to control closely allied troops before the change of Romanian attitude, incorporating them to German units (something similar to what happened with the Hungarian troops). Before this, even the pro-German Ion Antonescu demanded independence for the Romanian troops so that they would not remain in any way under the German command. All this tense situation motivated that on April 12, a Romanian delegation negotiated secretly in Cairo with representatives of the USSR, the United States and Great Britain the possibility of signing the peace. Among the Soviet demands were the following:

- Rupture of relations with Germany and incorporation of the Romanian Armed Forces together with the Allied troops, including the Red Army.

- Reconstitution of the Russian-Romanian border of 1940.

- Reparations to the Soviet Union for the damages caused in the war.

- Guarantees of freedom of movement of the Soviet troops and the other Allied nations through Romanian territory, with the obligation of Romania to supply all their needs.

Evidently, the demands of the allies were great, something that motivated a new Romanian proposal on April 19. By the time Marshal Antonescu discovered these secret negotiations, he prevented any other type of contact with the Allies, reaffirming their presence within the Axis.

An important group of political personalities, the Army and the Romanian nobility saw a great danger for their country in the attitude of Antonescu, a reason why they began to plan a plot against him.

At the end of April 1944, the "Romania Mare" 1st Armored Division had the following units:
- 1st Tank Regiment:
    à 1st Tank Battalion (with three Tank Companies).
    à 2nd Assault Gun Battalion of (with three Companies).
    à 1 HQ squad.
- 3rd Vanatori Motorized Regiment.
- 4th Vanatori Motorized Regiment.
- 1st Motorized Artillery Regiment.
- Special Weapons Motorized Group (with the 8th Engineers Motorized Regiment and the Motorized Reconnaissance Group).
    - 1 Anti-tank Artillery Battalion.
    - 1 Antiaircraft Artillery Company.

The situation of the German troops in the Romanian front was not considered as easy for various reasons. One of them, which in the end was of great importance, was the dependence of the Romanian and Hungarian railway lines for the supply of the frontline (the ancestral enmity and distrust between Hungarians and Romanians despite being allies neither helped at all to improve this aspect). The withdrawal of the German troops during 1944 before the Soviet push had delayed them to the borders of Romania before the war, although at least they managed to establish a defensive line along the Dniester River called the Trajan Line (after the Soviet attack of the first of June the front became more stable towards the north of that line) except for two bridgeheads that the Soviets had managed to establish. A second defensive line was the Stefan Line, which was located behind the eastern section of the Trajan; although this one was much less prepared.

Behind these frontline defenses, Germans and Romanians had a second and more powerful defensive line in the rearguard. This line was in the gap left by two important natural defenses of Romania: the Carpathians and the Lower Danube. It was called the Focsani-Namaloasa-Braila (FNB) gap and extended for more than 80 kilometers with various fortifications following the path of the lower Siret River. The defensive lines before the world conflict were not in the eastern part of the country, but towards the border with its Hungarian neighbor.

On July 25, Friessner, the commander of the "North" Army Group (Heeresgruppe "Nord"), was appointed to the same position but in the "Southern Ukraine" Army Group (Heeresgruppe "Südukraine"). There, what he found was a growing sense of distrust in some of his troops towards his Romanian allies due to the growing discontent of the Romanians towards their leader Antonescu. In a way, the Germans thought that the Romanians even hoped the arrival of the Soviets to make a change of side and leave the Germans alone (we will see how in a few days that German fear would be fulfilled, but not all Romanian troops would go to the side of the Soviets).

But that was not the only problem that Friessner found when taking command of the "Southern Ukraine" Army Group, since he could also see how his Army Group was being used as a source of human and material resources to reinforce others Groups of Armies further north. So that his armored force was reduced to the 13th Panzer Division commanded by Generalleutnant Hans Tröger, the 10th Panzergrander Division. With only two German Armies and two Romanian Armies, the "Southern Ukraine" Army Group had to maintain a defensive line along some 645 kilometers with the equivalent of 23 German Divisions and 23 Romanian Divisions with some 800,000 men (of which slightly less than half were Germans). The disposition of the four Armies was as follows:

- In eastern Bessarabia: Group "Dumitrescu" composed of the 3rd Romanian Army (commanded by the General of Armatâ Petre Dumitrescu) and the 6th German Army (commanded by General Maximilian Fretter-Pico). He was entrusted with the mission of maintaining the defensive line in the lower Danube (except for the two existing Soviet bridgeheads). The 3rd Romanian Army was fortified along the Dniester River and the 6th German Army was positioned on the Stefan Line.

- In Bucovina and Moldova: the "Wöhler" Group was composed of the 8th German Army (commanded by General Otto Wöhler himself) and the 4th Romanian Army (commanded by the General of Corp de armatâ Mihail Racovita). The reserves in the "Wöhler" Group were the 1st Armored Division, the 18th Mountain Division, the 8th Infantry Division and the 20th Panzer Division. The Romanian 1st Armored Division was specifically a part of the tactical reserve of the 4th Romanian Army. The 4th Romanian Army took positions in the Trajan Line, while the 8th German Army positions in the northern Bessarabia were quite precarious in the face of the Soviet offensive.

At the beginning of April 1944, the Soviets had crossed the border between Ukraine and Romania, so they were immediately ordered to conduct an offensive towards the area of Iaşi and Chisinau (Jassy and Kishinev). According to Axworthy the Romanian troops began to prepare themselves, and for that, on April 7 the Detachment "Cojocaru" was quickly formed by the 8th Cavalry Division and sent to the frontline in Husi. The Detachment "Cojocaru" was constituted by the 12th Rosiori Motorized Regiment, 3 TACAM T-60 (belonging to the 62nd battery), the 3rd Motorized Artillery Regiment and several independent Infantry Battalions (this ad hoc unit remained in the front until June 30 when the 8th Motorized Cavalry Division was removed to complete its rebuilding). Meanwhile, the men and vehicles of the 2nd and 3rd Ukrainian Front began the offensive.

The combats that followed belong to the so called 1st Battle of Târgu Frumos and took place between the 9th and the 12th of April. In those combats, the defensive actions fell on the German troops belonging to the Grossdeutschland Division and the Romanians belonging to the 1st Guard Division and 7th Infantry Division without the Romanian Armored Unit taking any part in them. The result was favorable to the defenders who succeeded in repelling the Soviets of the city of Târgu Frumos. In these clashes there were many German commanders who distrusted the loyalty of Romanian troops and even suspected of specific agreements between Romanian and Soviet units (as Spaeter cites in his book).

The Soviets, despite the delay of the 1st Battle of Târgu Frumos, continued to subject the Romanian and German defenders to various probe attacks over the defensive positions of both the Wöhler Group and the Dumitrescu Group during the last week of April. On April 28, one of these attacks towards Iaşi was stopped thanks to the action of the 23rd Panzer Division and the German 79th Infantry Division.

A new Soviet attack directed towards Târgu Frumos took place on May 2, giving rise to the so-called 2nd Battle of Târgu Frumos. On May 4 we can consider that the front line was completely stabilized except for the hill 256, which was still in Soviet hands. Once again, the Grossdeutschland Division, at this moment together with the 24th Panzer Division, managed to repel the Soviets from Hill 256 on May 7. Several small attacks and counterattacks took place during the month of June in the Iaşi area. Târgu Frumos, getting mainly the Division Grossdeutschland to maintain the German-Romanian defensive system. This 2nd Battle of Târgu Frumos was a great defensive victory led by Von Manteuffel's Grossdeutschland, in which during three days of battle, the Soviets lost some 350 armored vehicles (in addition to some 200 damaged ones) and only 10 German tanks were lost.

Despite the new German defensive success, the Soviets were managing to test the Romanian-German defenses with a view to a final attack. Actually, the defensive positions did not seem to have enough capacity to resist the enemy in Bessarabia and the Conducator Ion Antonescu had warned him. For this reason, Antonescu (supported by Friessner) suggested to Hitler the convenience of withdrawing troops to Transylvania (with the Carpathians as a natural defense) and the FNB line; but this suggestion was rejected with the consequences that will later be seen. Meanwhile, the withdrawal of the troops of the Axis continued, and the evacuation of Crimea took place between the months of April and May 1944.

Initially, the 1st Armored Division was trained along with the 23rd Panzer Division, which possibly received at least 32 used T-4s between April and May. So, on July 5, the 1st Armored Division had 48 T-4s and 20 TAs (the 16 T-4 Armored Rapid Detachment plus the 32 received later). There is also controversy about the number of TA that the 1st Armored Division had, since according to some sources the 1st Tank Regiment had 40 TAs in July 1944, although only 22 were integrated into the Romania Mare, since the other 18 were being repaired or even in the training camp of Dadilov, who was thinking about creating a new assault gun Battery.

Comparing the "Romania Mare" with a German Panzer Division, the former was less powerful because it had fewer vehicles and fewer troops; in spite of which it became the most powerful Romanian unit.

The overall equipment of the "Romania Mare" was not complete when the Soviet offensive took place (it still lacked 22 vehicles between tanks and assault guns), so that on August 19 1944 it had the following armored vehicles: 48 T-4s (Pz. IVH), 12 TAs (StuG III Ausf.G), 24 TBs armored transports (SPW 250 or 251) and 12 ABs armored vehicles (Sdkfz 222). About this topic, there are sources that show that the Armored Division should receive a few TAs that had been borrowed by the Kirchner Group, also within the 57th Panzer Corps. Although still nowadays, it remains unknown if these TAs finally came to be returned to the Division.

For the anti-tank defense, the "Romania Mare" had: 28 75 mm anti-tank guns, 6 50 mm Pak 38 anti-tank guns and 8 47 mm anti-tank guns.

The Division also had: 36 heavy machine guns, 105 light machine guns, 12 20 mm anti-aircraft guns, 4 13.2 mm machine guns, 25 mm Hotchkiss model 1939 anti-aircraft guns, 9 60 mm model 1939 Brandt/Voina mortars, 6 81.4 mm mortars, 6 120 mm mortars, 9 flamethrowers, 12 105 mm model 1936 Schneider guns and 12 100 mm Škoda howitzers.

While rebuilding its armored forces, Romania also intended, albeit unsuccessfully, that the 5th and 8th Cavalry Divisions were first transformed into Motorized Cavalry Divisions and then converted into Armored Cavalry Divisions.

Despite its potential, the "Romania Mare" was always closely watched by the Germans. At the end of July, the Germans tried to persuade the Romanians with the fact that experienced German instructors belonging to the 20th Panzer Division should handle the Romanian armor in case of attack; to which the outraged Romanians refused the German offer. This was due to the bad relationship always existing between Germans and Romanians, increased by the existing rumors of the Romanian defection from the Axis. The relationship was so difficult that the German liaison officer with Romanian troops sent a report in August 1944 to his superiors saying that when the combat should begin, all tanks should be manned by Germans better than by Romanians. The Romanian answers were always contrary to the Germans, and consisted in requesting to the Germans the return of the armored vehicles of Romanian property that still had in its power the 20th Panzer Division crews.

Operationally, the Armored Division, upon reaching its deployment area was distributed as follows:

- A Group: with the 1st Tank Regiment and the Special Weapons Motorized Group.

- B Group: with the 3rd and 4th Vanatori Motorized Regiments. Commanded by Colonel Constantin Nistor.

Another magnificent view of the TACAM R-2 exhibited at the National Military Museum in Bucharest. There were never enough copies of this tank destroyer model in front; although 2 TACAM R-2s were still in service on April 20. 1945. [From public domain – by mircea87]

After Romania switches sides, the Romanian soldiers and armored vehicles were used by the Soviets in a lot of clashes against their former allies. In the picture we can see a Romanian MG-42 machine gun team in the combats for Czechoslovakia, March 1945. [Courtesy by Pusca and Nitu from worldwar2.ro from MMN]

Silhouette of the low-visibility "Michael Cross" used on Romanian armored vehicles after the accession to the throne of Michael I. [Drawn by the author]

Insignia of the "Michael Cross" with three colors, which was used to facilitate aerial reconnaissance of the Romanian armored vehicles. This was the insignia of the Romanian Royal Army from 1 May 1941 to 3 September 1944. [From public domain – by alexD]

Romanian national insignia used by Romanian armored vehicles from the beginning of World War 2 until June 1941. This consisted of a circle with the three colors of the Romanian national flag: red (ring on the outside) - yellow (ring on the middle) -blue (an inner disk). [From public domain]

A R-2 at the National Military Museum in Bucharest showing several insigns and numbers in the hull and turret. This armored vehicle of Czechoslovak origin manufactured by the leading company Škoda represented the first modern tank that was available to the Romanian Army. [Courtesy by Pusca and Nitu from worldwar2.ro]

Another view of the same R-2 tank at the National Military Museum. The badge with the Royal crest was used by the R-1 and the R-2, but during the war it was preferred to retouch it with a darker shade of paint to make it less visible in the battlefield. [Picture by Dragos Pusca and courtesy by Pusca and Nitu from worldwar2.ro]

Image of a prototype of the excellent Mareşal tank destroyer, where you can see its turtle silhouette. This tank hunter proved to have such good performance that Germany showed its interest in the acquisition of the Mareşal. [Courtesy by Pusca and Nitu from worldwar2.ro]

A Tun Anticar pe Afet Mobil R-2 or TACAM R-2 tank destroyer in the National Military Museum in Bucharest. The blue horizontal stripe painted on the middle of the armored hull was possibly the marking of an unit commander. The use of the TACAM R-2 in combat began in July 1944 in the 63rd Tank Destroyers Company. [Picture by Victor Nitu and courtesy by Pusca and Nitu from worldwar2.ro]

The TACAM T-60 tank-destroyers were painted in Khaki color when they got out the Army Arsenal workshops in Bucharest. All TACAM T-60s in service with the Romanian Army had to be returned to the USSR in October 1944. [Courtesy by Pusca and Nitu from worldwar2.ro]

Several TACAM T-60 during the parade in Bucharest on May 10, 1943. This tank hunter had a crew of three men: driver, commander-gunner and loader. [Courtesy by Pusca and Nitu from worldwar2.ro]

A T-4 with a T-3 behind. 11 T-4 (and 11 T-3) were received a few days before the start of the Soviet offensive in November 1942 against Stalingrad. 10 T-4 were sent to the 1st Romanian Armored Division 1st Tank Regiment, although the T-4 in the photo was the only one that was not sent to Stalingrad and was kept for training duties in Romania. [Courtesy by Pusca and Nitu from worldwar2.ro]

The T-3 tank was the German Panzerkampfwagen III Ausf. N with short low speed 75 mm KwK L/24 gun. Romania acquired 11 T-3s in November 1942, of which 10 belonged to the 1st Tank Regiment. [Courtesy by Pusca and Nitu from worldwar2.ro]

Another photo of the Sd.Kfz. 9 FAMO tractor at the National Military Museum in Bucharest. These powerful vehicles towed the main guns that Romania had. [From public domain – by mircea87]

Several Mountain soldiers on a T-38 tank (in Germany the name was Pz.Kpfw. 38(t)) allowing to see the Michael Cross in the turret. The 50 T-38s that Romania received went to Crimea because the German interest of use them in that Front. [Courtesy by Pusca and Nitu from worldwar2.ro from MMN]

Cares de Lupta Tip R-35 or R-35 tanks belonging to the 2nd Tank Regiment alongside other vehicles in Bucharest, 1940. These tanks were from different origins because 41 R-35 were purchased from France and 34 R-35 came from Polish Batalion Czołgów Lekkich because they were interned in Romania while they flew from the Germans in 1939. [Courtesy by Pusca and Nitu from worldwar2.ro]

A Vanatorul de care R-35 after the combats in the last days of the war. This tank hunter has a 45 mm anti-tank gun and is bearing the Star over a white circle insign used by the 2nd Tank Regiment. [Courtesy by Pusca and Nitu from worldwar2.ro and tankarchives]

Painted by Arkadiusz Wróbel

TAs/StuG. III Ausf. G, II Battalion, 2nd Tank Regiment, Czechoslovakia and Austria 1945. We can see the new insignia consisting of a five pointed red star on a circular white background that was displayed by the Romanian armored vehicles belonging to the 2nd Tank Regiment.

TAs/StuG. III Ausf. G, 2nd Tank Regiment, Czechoslovakia and Austria 1945. This TA was painted in green as other Soviet armored vehicles. We recognize it as Romanian because the five pointed red star on a circular white background. In the fighting of the last days of the war, a large part of the Romanian armored vehicles were destroyed or were left out of service because they did not receive spare parts.

T-4/Pz.Kpfw. IV Ausf. J, Czechoslovakia 1945. One of the last Romanian T-4s still fighting in the last days of the war. When the WW2 ended, only one T-4 was still working. The Soviets forced the Romanians at the end of World War II to hand over the few armored vehicles that were still in service and later they dissolved the Romanian 2nd Tank Regiment.

Jagd.Pz. IV L48, 1st Armored Brigade 1945. Romania after the war received several JgPz.IV/70 tank destroyers from the Red Army (war booty). This 75 mm anti-tank gun armored vehicle was almost obsolete in the years after the war and they were officially known as TAs T4 in the army inventory and were used until 1950.

- C Group: with the 1st Motorized Artillery Regiment and the anti-tank and anti-aircraft artillery guns. Commanded by Colonel Alexandru Constantinescu, who in turn was the 1st Motorized Artillery Regiment chief.

In addition, the 1st Armored Division had under its command a German unit, the "Major Brausch" Detachment. This unit was formed by a Company with 10 StuG IIIs and a Motorized Infantry Battalion. According to some historians, those 10 StuG IIIs were actually Romanian TAs that before the lack of instructed crews had to be yielded to the Germans so that they could handle them. According to others, they were simply the StuG IIIs belonging to the 268th German Assault Gun Brigade.

The 1st Armored Division Swan Song

According to Nitu, Pusca, Axworthy and Zaloga we know that During June and July Romanians suffered a tense wait for the great Soviet offensive without any significant change in the frontline. On the left from Kuty to Iaşi the 8th German Army and the 4th Romanian Army maintained the sector; the 6th German Army positioned itself from the east of Iaşi to the Dniester river (in Dubossary) and from there following the course of the river to Tiraspol (near a Soviet bridgehead), where they were linked with the left wing of the 3rd Romanian Army following the lower course of the river. Two rivers, the Prut and the Siret, cut the geography of the area following a path from the north to the south, favoring in some aspects the defense of the area.

On August 8, an aerial reconnaissance carried out by Axis troops located an important movement of Soviet troops to the east of the Prut River, so it was perceived in the atmosphere that an attack would soon occur. Given the great danger they were suffering and realizing that the war was lost for Germany, during the month of August, various contacts between Romanian and Soviet officials took place through the front line.

Finally, the attack for the invasion of Romania was shared by 2 Soviet Fronts coordinated by Marshal Timoshenko, who were deployed along a frontline of about 400 kilometers:

- 3rd Ukrainian Front: commanded by Marshal Fyodor Tolbukhin and deployed in the left front area next to the Black Sea.

- 2nd Ukrainian Front: commanded by Marshal Rodion Yakovlevich Malinovsky and deployed on the right side of the Soviet attack front.

The number of men and vehicles was vastly superior to that of the defenders and consisted of 6 Mechanized and Armored Corps, 90 infantry divisions, about 1400 tanks and self-propelled guns and about 900,000 men (according to Muñoz, 1850 tanks and self-propelled guns and 929,200 men). In addition, Soviet ground troops received air support from some 1700-1850 aircrafts.

The defenders had a large deficit of tanks and aircrafts. The number of tanks ready on August 19 for the combat in the "Southern Ukraine" Army Group (Heeresgruppe "Südukraine") was approximately 120, with more than half Romanians (in addition to about 280 mainly German assault guns). The main armored formations were the 10th Panzer Grenadier Division (43 StuG IIIGs + 3 Pz.IIIMs possibly) and the 13th Panzer Division (with about 40 Pz.IVH/Js and about 20 StuGs).

The Soviet attack plan aimed for an advance in depth of about 200 kilometers and consisted of launching the 2nd Ukrainian Front in the area of the link between the Groups "Wöhler" and "Dumitrescu" in the northwest of Iași to separate them. After achieving this, they would head towards Vaslui and Falcui following the Prut River. Next, the 2nd Ukrainian Front should link up with the troops of the 3rd Ukrainian Front in the Kagul area (after having rolled over the defenses of the 3rd Romanian Army on the Dniester River and moving towards Tiraspol and Bendery to continue towards Huși). Thanks to this pincer attack breaking the Romanian defenses, the two Ukrainian Fronts would manage to pocket the powerful 6th German Army (after taking the crosses over the river Prut in the German rearguard) to finally annihilate all the Axis troops in the area between Chisinau and after reaching these objectives the new direction of the attack would be the defensive line Focsani-Namoloasa-Braila (FNB), to finally go to Ploiești and Bucharest, while the Black Sea Fleet would also collaborate with the flank of the attack.

Once it crossed the Dniester River, the Red Army reached Romanian land, where both Romanians and Germans had created a new defense line, which is where the 1st Romanian Armored Division was assigned; specifically, between Răscăeti and Palanca, in the north of Roman just behind the frontline. Together with the 268th German Assault Gun Brigade and the "Kessel" Group, the 1st Armored Division formed under the wardship of 57th Panzer Corps a rapid intervention force to act in any area in the defensive sector of the 4th Army. In the area of the 3rd Army, the only Romanian troops with tanks was the 1st Cavalry Division that had 2 R-35 Companies (possibly with 10 units per Company) that were mainly used as stationary artillery.

A certain fact is that the number of armor vehicles acquired by "Romania Mare" were not the same which it had in service. A significant number of the armor acquired from Germany were in the Mechanized Training Center (the 1st Armored Training Division). To the Mechanized Training Center, 14 T-4s, 2 T-3s and 5 TAs were transferred on the first of August 1944 (before the Soviet offensive). Apart from the armored vehicles that were in Romanian training camps, there are sources that place the tanks and assault guns that were not in service within the Romanian Army in German units. On August 11, the 1st Armored Division was ordered to advance towards the frontline and had to leave behind 16 TAs in the meeting area of the 20th Panzer Division; likewise, 23 T-4s and 7 TAs were left in charge of

German instructors for the formation of the 2nd Armored Division. Also, some other source tells us that about 30 T-4s and 21 TAs belonging to the 8th Romanian Cavalry Division could have ended up in the ranks of the German 13th Panzer Division by August 20 1944. The cause would be the one previously mentioned, the absence of an adequate number of Romanian crews trained to handle the T-4 and TA. It is really very difficult to verify these hypotheses; although a transfer of Romanian armored vehicles towards German units surely could have taken place in those days of summer 1944.

About the armored vehicles that already had more service time in the Romanian Army, we will try to "locate" them in the summer of 1944. The expected TACAM R-2, in August 1944, had not yet completed their training process (although 21 TACAM R-2s were delivered to the 63rd TACAM Company in the middle of 1944, only 10 copies were in the Dadilov training center), so they could not count on them. The R-35s that were not deployed with the 1st Cavalry Division were 20-30 (although we recall their limited fighting capacity for 1944, which is why they were used mainly as stationary artillery). As earlier mentioned, some of them were in the process of transformation to its version equipped with the 45 mm cannon (R-35/45) since 1943, so they also had no possibility of intervening in the combat in August (several copies were delivered to the 2nd tank regiment in the middle of 1944, so the adaptation and training process could not be completed before the Soviet offensive). The 5 T-38s that the Romanian armored arsenal still had were also out of service in the summer of 1944. Finally, the 16-18 TACAM T-60s that were not deployed with the "Romania Mare" 1st Armored Division were in process of being assigned to the 2nd Tank Regiment; and therefore, they were also not available for immediate shipment to the front. What can be considered as an irrefutable fact is that the "Romania Mare" 1st Armored Division was not yet complete on August 20.

It should also be remembered that in the middle of August, the 8th Motorized Cavalry Division was in the process of becoming the 2nd Armored Division (theoretically having to be equipped with two companies of 28 T-4s each and 6 T-As). Although in reality, this unit consisted of the 4th Rosiori Armored Regiment (with 23 T-4s and 7 TAs), the 12th Rosiori Motorized Regiment and the 3rd Motorized Artillery Regiment.

The Soviet troop movement in the vicinity of Iași and Târgu Frumos detected on August 16th by the troops belonging to the "Wöhler" Army Group indicated that the attack was imminent. Once the Red Army troops were in their positions, the action was very near since the Soviet roller advanced without pauses and it would go directly towards where the "Romania Mare" was. At 07:40 AM on August 20 1944, the Soviets began the so-called "Operation Iași-Kishinev" after an hour and a half of intense artillery preparation. Huge numbers of Soviet armor made a battering ram against the weak Romanian defenses. The 2nd Ukrainian Front unleashed the attack in northwest Iaşi (where it met the 4th Romanian Army), while the 3rd Ukrainian Front in the southern area of Tiraspol did the same (where the 3rd Romanian Army was). Specifically, on the Iaşi front, the artillery attack smashed the defensive lines of the 5th Romanian Infantry Division; to subsequently unleash the attack of the powerful 27th Soviet Army (which had 155 tanks and assault tanks). The results of the attack were immediate and at 12:30 PM the 27th Army captured Podu Iloaiei.

Although there is no intervention of Romanian tanks in eastern Bessarabia, we will comment that the Soviet attack of the 3rd Ukrainian Front against the "Dumitrescu" Group began at 08:20 AM on August 20 after one hour and forty-five minutes of artillery fire. As we can see, the attacks of the two Ukrainian Fronts got coordinated to completely saturate the Romanian-German defensive lines, as they finally achieved it.

The main attack carried out by Malinovsky´s 2nd Ukrainian Front was sustained by the 6th Tank Army and the 27th, 52nd and 53rd Soviet Armies of northwestern Iaşi. The initial attack was carried out by the 6th Tank Army, followed by the 27th Army. Meanwhile in the north of Târgu Frumos the 7th Guard Army and the "Gorshkov" Mechanized Cavalry Group positioned themselves along the Siret River to start another attack. Soon, Iaşi was in the hands of the Soviets and Târgu Frumos was in danger of being captured as well. The brutal Soviet attack caused that, in the first hours, it was reported within the "Wöhler" Army Group that 5 Romanian divisions were falling apart, leaving an important gap in the Romanian-German defensive system.

Focusing on the actions in which the Romanian 1st Armored Division was involved, the events that will be narrated below have as protagonists the Soviet troops of the 2nd Ukrainian Front. At night, on August 19-20, in prevention against an upcoming Soviet attack, the 1st Armored Division headed towards the towns of Goesti, Crucea and Sinesti, about 10-14 kilometers southeast of Podu Iloaiei. Inevitably, when the powerful Soviet attack was unleashed, the defensive line was broken in the Bahlui valley, between the towns of Baltati and Letcani (only the 18th Mountain Division opposed resistance in the wooded hills behind Bahlui). Due to the emergency, "Romania Mare" 1st Armored Division was sent at 2:00 PM to try to stop the Soviets with a counterattack with the main attack directed towards Hoisesti against the Soviet outposts of the 6th Tank Army that progressed to the south of Podu Iloaiei.

Before commenting on the events that took place in the Romanian 1st Armored Division, we remember what happened to the armored vehicles of the 1st Cavalry Division and of the 2nd Armored Division. The 1st Romanian Cavalry Division was integrated into the 3rd Romanian Army and was equipped with the obsolete R-35. In the attempt to stop the Soviet attack, they tried to maintain their positions in the Kogalnik River, but were eventually overtaken by the Soviet armor, losing themselves in the subsequent battles. On its part, the incomplete 2nd Armored Division according to Axworthy shortly after the Soviet attack in August was sent to the Tecuci area in the strategic zone of the Focsani gap. The armored forces of the 4th Rosiori Regiment (which we remember was part of this Division) originally belonged to the 1st Armored Regiment 2nd Battalion but with German instructors instead of Romanian crews. Finally, there were only 7 T-4s and 14 TAs who came to join the 4th Rosiori Regiment in Tecuci. The Romanian 2nd Armored Division could take very little part in the fighting, since on August 22 the "South Ukraine" Army Group HQ ordered the German instructors belonging to the 20th Panzer Division to take charge of all the T-4s and TAs from the 2nd Armored Division in Tecuci. With the loss of these armored vehicles, the 2nd Armored Division was renamed as the 8th Motorized Cavalry Division.

Returning to our main theme, it is important to keep in mind that the "Romania Mare" was not deployed as an only Unit in the same location, but was deployed in different combat groups: on the one hand the 1st Tank Regiment, on the other hand the 3rd Regiment Motorized Vanatori (reinforced with the 1st Assault Tank Company 1st Tank Regiment commanded by slt. Constantinescu) and finally the 4th Vanatori Motorized Regiment (reinforced by the 3rd Assault Tank Company 1st Tank Regiment commanded by Captain Grabinski). The units from C Group, such as the 1st Motorized Artillery Regiment and the anti-tank and anti-aircraft artillery guns, would be deployed on the 22nd between the two Vanatori motorized regiments.

The first need for the Romanians was to locate the area from where the Soviets could launch their attack. It is true that in the Germano-Romanian front line, the areas preferred by the Soviets to attack and where they therefore accumulated more troops, were those defended by the Romanians (in a way, the tactic used in Stalingrad was to attack the troops of the Axis in their weakest points, since they knew the low morale of a big group of the Romanian units that could fall apart as soon as the Soviet attacks began). In this way it facilitated the success of the penetration and also allowed the envelopment and subsequent siege of the most powerful units, as was the case of the Germans. In relation to this aspect and according to Axworthy 50% of riflemen divisions, 50% of artillery divisions and 80% of 2nd Ukrainian Front tanks would concentrate their attack on August 20 against a front line of 16 kilometers defended precisely for the 5th and 7th Romanian Infantry Divisions. On August 17, the 4th Army HQ warned that the enemy forces against the Germans were much weaker than those facing the Romanians. For this reason it was very important for the Romanians to know with the maximum accuracy any movement of the Soviet troops. For this reconnaissance mission the Reconnaissance Motorized Group commanded by Captain Ionescu was chosen. This unit departed from its location in Doljesti, coming into contact shortly after with Soviet troops who repelled them. Thanks to the information obtained in the recognition of the enemy, the decision was made to send the same August 20 to the "Romania Mare" against the enemy, making a counterattack on the flank of the Soviet advance that had broken the defensive line.

So the 3rd Vanatori Motorized Regiment and the 1st Tank Regiment were sent against the Soviet vanguard, positioning the first one to the west and the second to the east. For its part, the 4th Vanatori Motorized Regiment should take positions on the right flank.

We will relate separately the various movements that these three formations of the Romania Mare had during day 20 and the days immediately following; although evidently all these facts overlapped in that reduced space of time and we will link the facts of some groupings with those of others.

We started with the 3rd Vanatori Motorized Regiment commanded by Colonel Ion Ivan was ordered to leave from his base in Iugani towards the Siret River, which was crossed by the town of Miclauseni. As we mentioned earlier, this unit was reinforced with 1st Assault Gun Company of the Slt.Constantinescu; it was in Miclauseni where the TAs were attached to the Vanatori. Once reinforced with the TAs, crossing the Frumoasa valley, they headed towards the town of Podu Iloaiei. It would be there where (like the 1st Tank Regiment) they would contact the Soviet vanguard about 10.00 a.m. immediately the troops dismounted from their vehicles and proceeded to take defensive positions deployed west of the 1st Tank Regiment.

At the same time, the other units from the "Romania Mare", the 4th Motorized Vanatori Regiment under the command of Colonel Petrea, began its approach against the enemy vanguards. For this matter, they went to Miclauseni to cross the river Siret. They had been ordered to form the right flank of the troops belonging to the Motorized Brigade. In their approach, they reached the Bahlui valley to move later forward Zmeu, where they met with a powerful Soviet formation that forced them to retire quickly. Thanks to the artillery support of the C Group batteries assigned to the 4th Vanatori Motorized Regiment, they managed to stop the Soviets by separating their tanks from the infantry troops that supported them. This moment was used by the Vanatori to destroy several Soviet armors only with portable weapons in man-armored fighting. The Soviet unit, before the difficult situation that took the battle, preferred to leave and return to its previous locations.

For its part, the "Romania Mare" 1st Tank Regiment headed by Colonel Iliescu complied with the order received and sent its armor to the aforementioned flank of the Soviets. The intention was to be able to cut the enemy line, to isolate the Soviet outpost and to destroy it. But the reality was much more complicated, due to the inferiority in quantity and quality of the Romanian tanks against the Soviets. In addition, the 1st Tank Regiment, as we have said, was reduced in terms of its potential, as it had assigned two assault gun companies to the Vanatori Regiment; and having left his 2nd Assault Gun Company headed by Captain Alexe as the one in charge of protecting the approaching flank of the Tank Regiment in the area of Zmeu Obrejeni. So that only the T-4s belonging to the HQ Squad and the Tank Battalion was ready for the attack, not being able to use any TA. They were moving toward the Crucea hill, which allowed the observation of the Bahlui valley. But they were subjected to a heavy artillery fire, which with the loss of radio contact with the motorized reconnaissance group, caused the Romanian counterattack to be slowed down. Once the attack of the Soviet artillery was over, the T-4s continued their journey toward Podu Iloaiei.

It was around 10 am when the Romanian vanguard met with a formation of tanks belonging to the Soviet vanguard one kilometer south of Scobalteni. But the surprise for the Romanians was that they were not facing a flank of the Soviet approach, instead, they came up against the Soviet approach line.

The disposition on the terrain of both armored forces was approximately this: The Rumanians were unfolded immediately on both sides of the highway that united Doroscani with Podu Iloaiei, where until that moment its advance had advanced. On the other hand, the Soviets were in the surroundings of the mentioned community of Scobalteni.

The valiant Romanians, even knowing their numerical inferiority and the suicide of their confrontation with the Soviets, pushed themselves against the enemy. The first unit that did it was the 1st Tank Regiment 1st Battalion 1st Company headed by cotenant Velican, since it was in a position that gave them some advantage against the enemies. Evidently, the Soviet response did not wait, and a heavy fire of tanks and anti-tank guns came from Scobalteni, which damaged and immobilized three 1st Company T-4s; so the attack of Lieutenant Velican´s Company had to be re-converted into a defensive position in anticipation of the imminent Soviet attack.

For their part, the 2nd Company (commanded by Captain Grigorescu) and the 3rd Company (commanded by cotenant Vasilescu) also joined the battle. These two men would be considered missing after the fighting that day.

The situation became more difficult for the Romanians every minute more, as the powerful heavy tanks Josif Stalin 2 (JS-2) made their appearance in combat for the first time. Four of these armored monsters headed towards the Romanian lines, confident in the thickness of their armor. But the T-4 75mm guns from Velican Company along with those of the 2nd Company managed to destroy the four JS. In spite of this, the Soviets continued with repeated attacks against the armored vehicles of the 1st Company, which they even managed to surround.

The Soviet attacks didn't stop, but the Romanians managed to stay in their defensive positions. Around 2:00 pm, a Romanian TB Company (SPW 250) managed to join the conflict zone to support the armored vehicles. These same TBs were used to evacuate the wounded, whose number was growing continuously.

Simultaneously to the Soviet clash with the T-4s, also the 2nd Assault Gun Company TAs were involved in hard confrontations. An assault gun squad and a Soviet tank company trying to surround the Romanian T-4s on the left flank ran into the 2nd Assault Gun Company near Obrejeni (at that time headed by the cotenant Petrescu). The clashes between the two small armored formations resulted in a small Romanian victory, as they defeated much of the Soviet armor. Despite this, they could not avoid the TAs. Finally, Soviet armored formations managed to force the left flank of the 1st Tank Regiment, in order to surround them. The tenacious resistance opposed by the Romanian armor in its counterattack did not go unnoticed by the Soviet High Command, who recognized the great combativeness of the Romanians.

On their side, the men belonging to the 3rd Vanatori Motorized Regiment, due to the powerful Soviet combat force that was in front of them, began to lose their defense against the Soviets. What finally ended in a retreat in combat during the evening of that same day (August 20) under intense enemy artillery fire that tried to annihilate the defenders.

Due to the withdrawal of the Vanatori, the tanks belonging to the 1st Regiment began to be surrounded. In addition, the disgruntled Soviet commanders, observing the big resistance that the 1st Tank Regiment was doing, decided that three planes would send smoke bombs on the Romanians. This happened around 7:00 pm and the Romanian tanks still managed to stand firm in their positions thanks to the support of the TBs and to have been able to be supplied with ammunition up to four times. But the effect of the smoke bombs was used for another Soviet attack, which reached the road where the Romanian tanks were deployed, which were unable to shoot the enemy cause of the fear of shooting their own soldiers. The Romanian situation became desperate when the Soviet armor managed to surround the bulk of the Armored Regiment at dusk; reason why due to the complications of keeping its positions, it forced the Rumanians (the 7 T-4s belonging to the Company of Velican was there too) to break the fence in which they were and to retreat.

The battle for Scobalteni of the 1st Tank Regiment had lasted for about ten hours, causing both sides a large number of casualties. In fact, it is estimated that some 34 armored vehicles (between T-4 and TA) had been lost by the Romanians at nightfall on the 20th. On their side, the Soviets lost at least 60 tanks, among which there were a few exemplars of the modern JS. The commander-in-chief of the 4th Romanian Army informed his General Staff of the extreme difficulty encountered by "Romania Mare" in its counterattack and the sequential withdrawal of its various units.

The resignation of the Romanian armored unit was possible thanks to the darkness of the night. To increase the chances of escape, after having regrouped on one side of the road, the senior officers made the decision to divide their armored vehicles into two columns of departure. It was during this meeting that radio reports were received from the British BBC, which ensured that the Romanian 1st Armored Division had been completely destroyed or captured by the Soviets in those battles. Fortunately for the Romanians, the news was not true, since it was still able to fight a good part of the Romanian armored unit. Due to the losses suffered, the 2nd Tank Company was commanded by slt. Ion Dumitru (who became one of the best Romanian tank commanders, stating that at least he destroyed a Soviet tank during the fighting that day, although at the cost of immobilizing his own T-4) and the 3rd Tank Company under the cotenant command Stoenescu. The 1st Tank Company was still under the command of cotenant Velican.

Also thanks to the protection of the darkness, that same night the men belonging to the 3rd Vanatori Motorized Regiment managed to escape. Although due to the confusion (and as it would happen with the men belonging to the 1st Tank Regiment), the unit broke down into small groups. The most outstanding of these groups was one of its battalions, that under the direction of the lieutenant colonel Gheorghe Rascanescu was able to break the contact with the enemy while also it did it with the rest of its Regiment, going towards Madarjac. During its journey, it was reinforced by other troops that were retreating, such as those of the 1st Artillery Motorized Regiment (with some of its artillery batteries) or some TA (very possibly belonging to the 1st Assault Gun Company of the slt. Constantinescu that was assigned to the 3rd Regiment). This growing formation directed by Rascanescu assumed the responsibility of creating a new defensive line that followed the disposition of these localities: Manastirea de Sud-Bojila-Frumusica-Madarjac-Slobozia. From this line, they wanted to slow the Soviet advance down at least the time necessary to allow the rest of the Romanian units in full retreat, they managed to reach territory controlled by the Romanians.

Meanwhile, at dusk on the 20th, Colonel Petrea, faced the growing Soviet thrust and ordered the 4th Vanatori Motorized Regiment to retreat to the Trei Parale forest. The journey, although not very long, was difficult due to the low visibility and the danger of the approach of the Soviet armored formations that stalked the retreating Romanians. Upon reaching the area of the Trei Parale forest, the Vanatori were deployed, taking defensive positions that they would maintain during August 21, trying to slow the Soviet approach as much as possible. This time the Romanians tried to empty as much as possible the weapons deposit that they had in the forest and that seemed like a priority to be able to maintain some fighting capacity.

As we have mentioned, the retreat of the surviving tanks from the 1st Tank Regiment (led by Velican, Dumitru and Stoenescu) started around 23.30 on August 20 and took place in the first hours of August 21 (taking advantage of the complete darkness of the night) in two tanks columns marching cross-country with the 7 BT survivors between the two columns. The withdrawal route that had been set was Scobalteni-Harpasesti-Madarjac-Ghidionu-Roman. But it was inevitable that they would be detected by the Soviets who wandered the area in search of Romanian armor. So when they tried to surround the town of Harpasesti, the Romanian armor was subjected, in the proximity of Doroscani, to a large fire from Soviet tanks that fired blindly due to the darkness of the night. Fortunately for the Romanians, they did not suffer significant damages and could continue advancing, shortly after that they lost contact with each other (approximately in the area of Mardarjac) due to the darkness of the night, not being able to help with any type of lighting that could help the Soviet troops. So one of the columns (the one led by the Ion Dumitru with the armored vehicles of the 2nd Company) was composed of 13 T-4s and 3 TBs; while the other was composed of the HQ Platoon, the armored from the 1st Company with Velican in front and some of the 3rd Company tanks.

The column commanded by Dumitru, when lost the contact with the other armored column went towards the Sinesti, where they arrived at 02:00 am. There they found a patrol of soldiers belonging to 4th Vanatori Motorized Regiment. They were informed about the difficult situation they had in Stornesti, where soldiers belonging to their Vanatori Company were resisting Soviet attacks. This Vanatori Company was the rearguard of the 4th Vanatori Motorized Regiment and had been left behind to ensure the evacuation of the weapons deposit that the Romanian troops had in the Trei Parale forest. Meanwhile, the bulk of the Regiment had begun its withdrawal southward.

While this was happening, the detachment commanded by Lieutenant Colonel Gheorghe Rascanescu ordered to continue the withdrawal of the bulk of his troops and they arrived in Madarjac on the night of the 20th and early morning of the 21st. He formed a new defensive line near Madarjac that allowed gaining time for the retreating troops to be able to move away from the Soviets.

For its part, the column Velican with the remains of the 1st and 3rd Companies ended up heading towards the town of Madarjac, where they arrived at dawn on the 21st.

It was then in Madarjac where the column commanded by Velican met with the troops of the Detachment commanded by Lieutenant Colonel Rascanescu, who managed to form with his 7 T-4s an armored group composed of about 20 T-4s and about 10 TAs. Although this new "ad hoc" formation could have some operational capacity, it was burdened by the lack of ammunition after the intense fighting sustained only a few hours before. In spite of the Romanian logistical difficulties, Lieutenant Colonel Rascanescu achieved that around 15.00 pm on 21st, the armored vehicles were loaded with ammunition in order to be operational again. According to some source (although not confirmed), they did not wait for the order to move towards Voinesti, where armored enemy formations had already been detected. The 30 armored vehicles commanded by Rascanescu would have been launched against at least 50 Soviet tanks with their corresponding infantry attachment, which after a violent exchange of fire, managed to repel towards 9 - 10 pm from Voinesti. Whether this Romanian attack is completely true or not, what is certain is that the armored troops in charge of Rascanescu went into combat several times against the Soviets trying to stop their advance in the area of Madarjac. As expected, the Soviets went on the counterattack, needing at least three successive raids to finally expel the Romanian troops from the Madarjac area. In these confrontations that ended with the withdrawal of the Romanians on the area of Bara Targ, the cohesion of the unit headed by Rascanescu would be lost, returning to roam just some small Romanian armored formations, such as the 7 T-4s under Velican command. Shortly after to the T-4s commanded by Velican, 3 TAs were added, which they went towards Pildesti with. They arrived on the 23rd as will be related later. For its part, the bulk of the Vanatori continued their route to Lugani, a locality they found unprotected; motivated by the fact that Rascanescu at dusk of August 21 organized a new defensive line that blocked the road between Roman and Pazcani as well as the passage of the Siret river through the town of Miclauseni.

Other small armored Romanian formations belonging to the "Romania Mare" after being isolated tried to reach safer territories. One of them was formed by a small indeterminate number of armored vehicles under the command of Lieutenant Colonel Gheorghe Matei from the 1st Tank Regiment, which managed to make its way to Roman, following later on its withdrawal. Also, the remains of the 1st Assault Gun Company (under the command of Radu Constantinescu) or some armored vehicles from the 3rd Company (commanded by lt Stoenescu) had to retreat towards Roman, where they would arrive on August 22. For their part, the surviving TA belonging to the 2nd Assault Gun Company also managed to retire on their way to Madarjac and Bojila, which allowed them not to be annihilated by the great Soviet offensive. Another unit that is known to have marched alone fleeing from the Soviets, was the Motorized Reconnaissance Group, which is known to have arrived in Girov, on the afternoon on August 23 (later marched in the direction of Roznov to arrive on the afternoon on August 24 to Casin).

The movement of all these small armored groups is really complicated to follow, because of the lack of specific sources available, and because of the confused situation after the Soviet offensive was unleashed.

Before the imposing Soviet advance, as we have been able to appreciate, part of the Romanian units fought with boldness, although it is also true that others offered practically no resistance against the attackers. The critical situation in the entire front line caused the Trajan line to be irretrievably lost on August 21 (serve as an example of the Soviet breakthrough capacity, the more than 40 kilometers that had entered behind the Romanian defensive lines on 6th Guard Mechanized Corps). This fact motivated Friessner to notice the serious danger that the 6th Army would run if he did not retreat (as we discussed earlier the intention of the Soviets was to capture the crosses over the Prut River in the rear of the Germans and thanks to this maneuver, encircle them); order that he gave immediately. Faced with the accomplished facts and the success of the Soviet breakthrough, Hitler had to authorize the withdrawal towards the Focsani-Namaloasa-Braila line or FNB (what Antonescu had requested on repeated occasions during that summer of 1944); although, as the events showed, it was too late for that. On August 22 the Romanian 4th Army also received the authorization to give up under the Focsani-Namaloasa-Braila line, receiving the order to cover the withdrawal of the "Romania Mare", the Guard Division and the 4th Infantry Division (these last two units belonging to the V Corp).

We continue the narration with the armored group, due to the fact that we have more information about their movements. The column was directed by Dumitru; which we had left in Sinesti together with a Vanaori Company. At dawn on August 21, 25 German Stug IIIs belonging to the 286th Assault Gun Brigade appeared and headed towards the Romanian positions of the Vanatori in Sinesti. The Soviets, seeing the arrival of the German armored vehicles, deployed anti-tank artillery guns ready to kill them. But paying all their attention to the Germans, they did not notice the arrival of Dumitru's armored vehicles, which smashed them easily. In addition, they were also able to destroy four Ford trucks that lent support to the Soviet gunners. This confrontation was observed by General Korne, who contacted Dumitru and ordered him to surrender.

The small column commanded by Dumitru was reorganized under constant air attacks in the area of Bira-Boghicea and following the orders of General Korne, began its withdrawal and went to the town of Boghicea, where there was a 4th Vanatori Motorized Regiment Company and a 150 mm model 1934 Škoda howitzer Battery, which belonged to the 1st Heavy Motorized Artillery Regiment. These men had been deployed like the rearguard of the Regiment to slow the march of the Soviets and to provide an essential time for the bulk's withdrawal of the Vanatori unit (specifically, it belonged to the 4th Vanatori Motorized Regiment commanded by Colonel Petrea who, after having resisted in their positions in the Trei Parale forest, left after surviving a Soviet night attack in which the colonel was captured). Facing this situation and the imminent arrival of the Soviet armored units, Dumitru decided that his tanks would take defensive positions after the infantry troops and wait for the enemies. But before the Soviets arrived, coming from the Trei Parale forest, they reached the Romanian positions (with the remains of the Vanatori company that had been resisting in Stornesti), followed very closely by the Soviet outposts.

The reception that Dumitru's armor and the battery of howitzers gave to the Soviets caused many casualties and finally managed to force the attackers to surrender. At this moment Dumitru took advantage to chase them trying to cause as much damage as possible. Approximately one hour later, Dumitru and his men headed towards Bara Targ, where they were again waiting for the arrival of the Soviets, taking new defensive positions (between Bara Targ and Doljesti, Colonel Petrea from 4th Motorized Regiment Vanatori had tried to build defensive positions with Vanatori troops, before he was captured by the Soviets). They did not have to wait long, since from the Oteleni area, the Russian troops reappeared with such impetus and artillery power that, given the impossibility of maintaining their positions, in the early hours of August 22 Dumitru gave the order to retreat (at least the hours that had contained the Soviet forces allowed the remains of the Romanian Guard Infantry Divisions, 1st, 4th and 13th Infantry Divisions together with the 46th German Infantry Division to cross the Siret River in the morning of August 23). In their withdrawal, they had to cross the river Siret to later reach Roman (this town had become the checkpoint of the Romanian troops' withdrawal from the front because it was the best place to cross the Siret River), from where they went towards Sabaoani. There was a defensive strong point with anti-tank ditches guarded by a Romanian engineers Company supported by a German 100 mm howitzers Battery. The importance of this town was that from there the Romanians could control the road from the crossing area of the Siret River both by Miclauseni and by Adjudeni.

For its part, the 3rd Motorized Vanatori Regiment, which had taken positions late on August 21 in Lugani and Miclauseni, did not keep these longer since at dawn on August 22 they were ordered to go to the Onesti area. Immediately they left with the vehicles that still had in service towards Boizeni, and after a few hours reached the Onesti area after having crossed Moldova by Tupilati. The reason for the withdrawal order was the Romanian High Command attempt to gather the survivors belonging to the Regiment to try to turn it back into a fully operational unit despite the Soviets' victory. At dusk on August 22, the troops commanded by Rascanescu took defensive positions in Onesti, waiting for the arrival of more comrades. They did not have to wait too much, between the evening on August 22 and 23, small groups of Vanatori belonging to the 4th Motorized Vanatori Regiment began to appear, after having been decimated in the Trei Parale forest and Bara Targ, they escaped through Roman.

A few days later, the Romanian armored troops had been forced to retreat despite their brave attempt to stop the Soviets and then spread out towards the Romanian rearguard to join dispersed defensive positions such as Stornesti or Sabaoani. Trying to take action against this situation that further diminished the fighting capacity of the Romanian tanks, at dawn on August 23, Colonel Iliescu arrived at Sabaoani. There he spoke with Dumitru and assured him that in a few hours reinforcements would arrive to maintain that position. In fact, only a few hours later (around 11 am), the reinforcements promised by the boss of the 1st Tank Regiment, Colonel Iliescu, arrived, consisting in several trucks with supplies. In addition, at around 2 p.m., four German 75mm anti-tank guns arrived and that significantly increased the defensive power at Sabaoani. Meanwhile, the anti-tank ditch around the town was improved as much as possible. Despite the reinforcement of the German-Romanian positions in Sabaoani, orders were received claiming the Howitzer Battery in the town of Tupilati, so that suddenly, decreased the firepower of the defenders.

It did not take long to see if the locality had become a defensive strong point that could stop the Soviets because, at dusk, a Soviet armored formation composed of an armored column appeared on the horizon from the Rotunda-Adjudeni highway: 22 tanks with artillery support. This formation had been detected by the reconnaissance patrol in charge of the platoon commanded by slt. Vasile Ienceanu. This small Romanian formation had headed to Adjudeni and when they detected the Soviet armor they came back without being detected by these, informing about the troops arranged in Sabaoani.

Dumitru already aware of the critic situation had designed together with the defending troops a plan to turn into reality as soon as the Soviet formation arrived. Approaching about 100 meters from the anti-tank ditch, Romanian engineers caused the blasting of the roads leading to Sabaoani, forcing the Soviets to move through the open field and to dismount the infantry from their tanks. It was at that moment when tanks and infantry were thrown against the antitank ditch while having the sun completely in front of them, making it difficult to see the defender positions. For this reason the Soviets did not notice the presence of several T-4s and anti-tank guns in a forest located 700 meters from the anti-tank ditch, which received the order to shoot at them by Dumitru, and together with the troops that were in Sabaoani, they opened a heavy artillery fire that practically annihilated the enemy formation without giving them barely time to react. Possibly Dumitru destroyed one of the 22 enemy battle tanks, although due to the tense and confusion of the moment, it would be very difficult to confirm it. According to some source, during this confrontation, the Romanians received unexpected support from 3 German tanks and 2 StuG IIIs, which would be arranged in the easternmost part of the village.

The plan had worked, but it was just a small Soviet group, so that after the combat, the defending troops were again in position for new attacks although already without the tanks commanded by Dumitru, which received the order to move (in fact, the Soviets returned a few hours later with new reinforcements that finally forced the Romanians and Germans to retreat towards Pildesti). Just one hour after dismissing the Soviets, Dumitru's armored vehicles headed toward Gheraesti-Tetcani, then recessed for an hour and a half on the road between Falticeni and Roman. From there, they continued their march towards Dulcesti, although before getting there they had a pleasant surprise. It was in the town of Pildesti where they met with their comrades from the 1st Tank Regiment 1st Battalion 1st Company commanded by Locotenent Velican, whom they had lost contact with, in the Mardarjac area after the fighting held in Doroscani. As we discussed earlier, the armored column under the commanded by Velican only had 7 T-4s and 3 TAs; despite that, it meant an important reinforcement for the armored column commanded by Dumitru. Once the armored survivors belonging to the Romanian Tank Regiment joined, they headed towards the crossing of the Moldova River in Corhana; which crossed at midnight between August 23rd and 24th. When they arrived at the bridge, they saw a German artillery battery that was defending itself from the attack of a small Soviet unit, not allowing them to keep their march. The Romanian armored column made its appearance annihilating the Soviets and saving their German comrades from a difficult situation. After this small fight, they continued their route towards Dulcesti, during which they lost 1 T-4 and 1 TA due to mechanical failure, they abandoned and destroyed them. They progressed to a point about 2 km southwest of Dulcesti.

Switching Sides

The powerful Soviet advance on August 23 allowed the 6th German Army and the 4th Romanian Army to be surrounded by the two Soviet Fronts; the attackers reached the line between Târgu Neamt and Tatar-Bunar, only about 50-60 kilometers from the fortified line of the Focsani Gap. The Germans before this situation began to raise the possible Soviet advance towards Hungary. By mid-1944 some Romanian generals began to be tired of their German ally and collaborated in fighting them.

As we already mentioned and according to Nitu, Pusca and Axworthy the Romanian military conspirators knew that in Bucharest there were more German than Rumanian troops, highlighting among the latter the Royal Guard Calarasi Regiment with a mixture of armored vehicles (R-35, T-38, and FT-17) of little fighting value. But the events in the front line hurried in Romania very important political changes. On the afternoon on August 23, Conducator Ion Antonescu was arrested along with two of his ministers; for a short while later King Michael I solemnly announced on a radio transmission the formation of a new Government under the command of Constantin Sănătescu (who had been until January 1944 the commander-in-chief of the 4th Army). In addition, the end of the fighting was announced in Romania when all the troops received the order to stop the fight (at 00.30 am on August 24 the Romanian divisions belonging to the 4th Army formally received the cease-fire order with the Soviets); while negotiators were sent to the Soviet Union and to the Soviet commanders from the units that were in front of the Romanians troops. Although the initial answer from the Soviets to any desire for peace on the part of Romania, it always claimed the Romanian troops' surrender and their immediate "travel" to prison. The problem for the Romanian soldiers was that the Romanian change of side executed by the king without the direct approval of the Soviet Union forced the Soviets to capture the surrendered Romanian troops and to keep them as prisoners.

The German reaction was immediate and on August 24 German troops were ordered to head towards Bucharest to occupy the city and eliminate the troops loyal to the king. About 6000 men departed towards 07.30 am towards the Romanian capital, but in a few minutes, they were stopped by an important resistance from Romanian troops.

While resisting the Germans, the Romanian troops also initially received orders to occupy defensive positions in the Focsani-Namoloasa-Braila line against the Soviets. This line represented the most important defensive position in Romania and included some 160 kilometers of anti-tank ditches, trenches, minefields and some 1600 concrete bunkers. But shortly after the Romanian troops (and always with the intention of not disturb the Soviets) received the counterorder to take positions to the south of the Focsani-Namoloasa-Braila line (which was finally taken by the Soviets without Romanian opposition).

The Soviets belonging to the 2nd Ukrainian Front managed to occupy the city of Bacau on August 24, managing to cross the Siret River. Because the danger of being trapped, the 6th Army, Friessner start marching towards the Carpathians.

The withdrawal of the Romanian armor continued the next day, on August 24, when they met with a small German formation also in retreat. It was at that moment when the Romanians after a bloody and dizzying day in which they had maintained countless clashes with the Soviets, they learned that Romania had declared an armistice. It is estimated that the losses during the fight after the Soviet offensive of the "Romania Mare", in Moldova could reach 34 vehicles between T-4s and TAs (both by the action of the Soviets and by the German appropriation of some of the armored vehicles of Romanian property). On the positive side, he claimed the destruction of numerous enemy tanks (60 Soviet tanks only on August 20). With such a small number of casualties in their armored vehicles, it is reasonable to consider that the Romanian 1st Armored Division managed to escape from the fighting quite intact despite the losses and consequent disorganization following the Soviet attack.

On August 24 the Romanian 1st Tank Regiment armored column, already knowing the news of the armistice, continued its advance towards the south, seeking shelter within its own country. They crossed localities like Bozieni, Girov or Casin, until arriving at the bridge over the river Cracau in Roznov at dusk in the same day. Although the intention of the armored column was to cross immediately, the bridge was collapsed by a large number of Romanian troops belonging to the 1st Corps that were crossing it. They had to wait until the morning of August 25 to cross it and follow in the footsteps of the retreating infantry.

In their advance, they managed to meet with other tanks from the 1st Tank Regiment commanded by Lieutenant Colonel Gheorghe Matei, whom they found on the road (these tanks had managed to cross the river the day before from Roman); as well as some Tas belonging to the 1st Assault Gun Company commanded by slt. Radu Constantinescu (who had also spent a few hours earlier in the town of Roman). The increasingly powerful Romanian armored column reached the town of Tazlau on August 25, where they met the men belonging to the 7th Heavy Artillery Regiment, who had managed to get there by their own means. In spite of the several days of combat that the "Romania Mare" troops had maintained, the armored unit was quite intact given the difficult circumstances. Due to its still important firepower, the remains of the "Romania Mare" were ordered to go towards Bucharest to fight the Germans. Although the Romanians tried to continue their advance, the Soviet troops had already overtaken them and waited for them a little later on their route (the Romanian armored column was completely surrounded by the Soviets). When the meeting with their new "friends" took place, the Soviets forced them to stop their march while pointing their weapons at them. Once the Soviets examined the Romanian units that formed the retreating column, they were allowed to continue their advance to Frumoasa, where the same scenes were repeated a few hours earlier with the Soviets stopping the Romanian march under the threat of attack the Romanians if they did not obey. The tension between the Rumanians was increasing with such intensity, that in this occasion they did not accept the Soviet orders and defensive positions were taken. Given the way events were taking place, the Soviets chose to withdraw and immediately contact the Romanian 1st Corps HQ. Its leader, lieutenant-general Radu Gherghe, finally managed to decrease the confrontation with the Soviets, but only so that the next day they surrendered to the Soviets. And that's how on August 26 most of the Romanians belonging to the armored column commanded Lieutenant General Radu Gherghe were interned in a prison camp while their tanks and other vehicles were requisitioned and taken to Valea Lui Ion.

The Romanian military only had two alternatives (despite many attempts by the Romanian authorities to avoid both), either surrender and be turned into prisoners or in some cases join Soviet units and fight under their command. The following is what happened to a small part of the men belonging to the 1st Tank Regiment. These men were not interned, since for them the war was not over, their fate was the formation of the armored Detachment "Lt. Col. Gheorghe Matei". According to Pusca, Nitu, and Axworthy, this new armored unit was under the command of the former head of the 1st Tank Regiment, Lieutenant Colonel Gheorghe Matei, from whom he took the name. It was made up of:

- 1 Tank Company with 7 T-4s.
- 1 Assault Gun Company with 7 TAs.
- 1 Vanatori Motorized battalion.
- 1 Engineer Company.
- 1 Antiaircraft Artillery Company endowed with 25 mm model 1939 Hotchkiss guns.
- 1 Anti-tank Company endowed with 12 75 mm model 1943 Reșița guns.

The total number of the new group was of 1058 men and of 133 different types vehicles, that were assigned to the Soviet 7th Guard Army; the 1st Tank Regiment was officially dissolved because of the wishing of the Soviets.

Some men of the 1st Tank Regiment, like the slt. Dumitru, managed to escape avoiding momentarily the prison camp. In a short time, they were captured to be confined in the prison camp. Dumitru again managed to escape from his Soviet "allies" and arrive disguised as a peasant by secondary roads to the town of Târgoviste (where the Romanian Army Mechanized Training Center was located).

Almost simultaneously, on August the 24th, at the Târgoviste Army Mechanized Training Center (with vehicles from the same center), a new unit was created under the protection of the Soviets. It was the "General Nicolescu" Armored Detachment (also known as "Jupiter") and consisted of:

- 1 Tank Battalion: endowed with two Companies, battle tanks (with 10 T-4s) and assault guns(with 10 TAs).

- 1 TACAM Battalion: with 12 TACAM R-2s.

- 1 Vanatori Motorized Battalion (from the 4th Vanatori Motorized Regiment).

- 1 Reconnaissance Group (consisting of 1 Armored Vehicles Platoon and 1 Amphibious Vehicles Platoon).

- 1 Antitank Company: with 12 anti-tank 75 mm model 1943 Reșița guns.

A third formation that the Soviets authorized to create was the "Mr. Victor Popescu" Armored Detachment which was made of men and vehicles from the 1st Armored Training Division. It was made up of:

- 1 R-2 Tank Company.

- 1 T-38 tank Platoon.

- 1 R-35 tank Platoon.

- 1 Vanatori Motorized Unit.

- 1 Antiaircraft Battery.

- 1 Anti-tank Battery.

On the 25th, some 150 German planes bombed Bucharest, which finally determined the official declaration of war on Germany by Romanian side. Faced with the situation in Romania, Hitler realized that it was impossible to occupy the Focsani Gap with his troops (already in the hands of the Soviets), so he ordered on the 26th that 'Südukraine' Army Group retreat in the direction of the area of the Carpathians and take possession of several mountain passes.

Only two days had passed since Romania had signed the armistice and the Soviets were already planning the Romanian use in the last few months of the world conflict. Despite the fact that in the upper echelons of Romanian Command they tried to get their country considered as another ally, that possibility obviously did not occur precisely through Stalin's mind. In fact, they were going to allow the Romanians to take part in the fighting against the Germans and Hungarians (already in full retreat but still very dangerous, in fact after the defection of Romania, the IV Hungarian Corps was organized to block the advance of the Soviet and Romanian forces in the plains of southern Hungary in Arad and Lippa), but always under close guardianship by the Soviet side. As we have seen, the armored formations that the Soviets allowed keeping the Romanians were very small; so that they assured themselves that their capacity to act would always be subject to the decision of the Soviet High Command took. In fact, to further increase control over the Romanian armor, the "General Nicolescu" Armored Detachment and the "Lt. Col. Gheorghe Matei" Armored Detachment were merged a short time later in a new formation: the 4th Army's Armored Group (to which should offer armored support).

To facilitate the understanding of the small Romanian armored formations after the armistice, here we reflect a brief review of the Romanian armored units after the armistice.

- "Lt. Col. Gheorghe Matei": Armored Detachment formed with the remains of the 1st Armored Regiment after dissolving it.

- "General Nicolescu". Armored detachment: They got to participate in combats in Otopeni, Baneasa, and Bucharest; then to fight in Transylvania. They participated in clashes against his former allies as part of the "General Rozin" Moto-mechanized Corp.

- "Mr. Victor Popescu" Armored detachment Unit that was only active a few days, since it was created on August 24 and disbanded on August 31. In spite of this, he had the opportunity to participate in combats in the area of Ploiești aimed at preventing the withdrawal of the Germans towards Hungary.

- 2nd Tank Regiment. That was just over two months after the Romanian change of side and as agreed in the armistice, it finally became the only Romanian armored unit.

- 4th Army's Armored group (Grupul Blindat al Armatei 4 romane): formed on October 4, 1944, as a result of the merger of the armored detachments "General Nicolescu" and "Lt. Col. Gheorghe Matei".

Against The Ancient Allies

The change of side of Rumania had immediate consequences in the deployment of the troops of the Axis (Germany and Hungary), since just to the south of the Magyar country it was a quite unguarded zone (yes that there were some Hungarian troops arranged towards the south due to the Traditional distrust of the Hungarians towards the Romanians, it was considered necessary to control the mountain passes north of the region of Transylvania, and only a few days later, on September 5, 1944, the Hungarians launched an offensive against Romanian forces superior in number aiming to the north of Transylvania. The origin was the 2nd Magyar Armored Division and inside it the powerful 2nd Company of the Hungarian battleship Tarczay. They left after crossing the river Aranyos (Aries) in the direction of Torda at sunset on the 5th of September beginning the Magyar attack. The beginning of the Magyar offensive was a success since it managed to reach the town of Torda (Turda, today in Rumania) ten days after starting and finally crossing the Maros (Mures) rivers.

But the Romanian infantry troops united with Soviet troops and a Romanian armored group (the armored Detachment "General Nicolescu"), to which we must add the Armored Detachment "Lt. Col. Gheorghe Matei" which was subordinated to the 2nd Ukrainian Front (that took part in the actions in the southeast of Transylvania) were launched on counterattack.

One of the armored units that the Rumanians faced the Hungarians, was the Armored Detachment "General Nicolescu". This was deployed in Cornesti, already in Transylvania, in union with troops of infantry (9th Infantry Division) and cavalry (8th Motorized Cavalry Division) also Romanians. As we have already mentioned, the main rival with which they met was the 2nd Magyar Armored Division, which at least caused the destruction of two tanks in the vicinity of the aforementioned town of Cornesti. This locality in the hands of the Hungarians was taken on September 7 by the Hungarians. At that time (on the 8th) there was another attempt to take Cornesti by a small Romanian armored unit under the command of Captain Radu Balacescu supported by infantry troops, which managed to penetrate the town. They were subjected to anti-tank fire that immobilized the Romanian tanks and fired at their crew.

These confrontations made it clear that at that time, the Hungarian armored troops had greater combat capacity than their Romanian counterparts. This fact has to be justified by the greater experience of the Hungarian tankers.

In spite of this, the situation of the war for the Axis with the numerical superiority of the Romanian troops halted the Hungarians definitively on September 9 in their attempt to reach the mountain passages of northern Transylvania. When the Hungarian advance was slowed down, these faced the danger of being isolated behind the enemy lines after the powerful Soviet-Romanian offensive, decided to retreat behind the Maros River where they would form a defensive line whose main bastions were the populations of Torda and Aranyosegerbegy (Viişoara). The German-Magyar attempt to capture the mountain passes failed and the "door" was left open to attacks from the south and east against Hungary.

On September 13th the Hungarian troops carried out an attack advancing from the right flank of the front line from the Makó and Gyula region towards Arad, but two Romanian infantry and one cavalry divisions were awaiting such advance. Despite the initial resistance, the Hungarians came to occupy the city of Arad on the evening of September 13th with all its bridges intact (the Romanians did not try to defend the city at all costs, so they preferred to retreat to their defensive lines in the Maros river). On September 20th a joint Soviet-Romanian attack supported by 40-50 tanks broke the Hungarian defensive line. So that day 22 Arad was recovered by the Soviets-Romanians, only three days after a little further south they also took the city of Temesvár (Timisoara); to end the Soviet offensive in western Transylvania.

After taking the initiative on the Transylvania front, an attempt was made to regroup the small Romanian armored units, for which some of these were disbanded. As happened with the Armored Detachment "General Nicolescu", which was dissolved on September 28 or with the Armored Detachment "Lt. Col. Gheorghe Matei" also at the end of September (although this process had already begun with the dissolution of the Armored Detachment " Mr. Victor Popescu "on August 31).

As we have already mentioned, as a result of the consolidation of the units integrated into the Armored Detachments "General Nicolescu" and "Lt. Col. Gheorghe Matei", on October 1, 1944 the Battleship Group of the 4th Romanian Army was formed. This new unit had:

- A tank battalion consisting of three companies. A company with 10 T-4, another with 8 TA and the third with 16 TACAM R-2.

- One Battery (the 62nd) with TACAM T-60.

- A reconnaissance company consisting of 5 AB vehicles, one SPW 250, several Horch vehicles and a Schwimmwagen section.

- A Vanatori motorized battalion.

- A heavy artillery motorized battalion.

- An anti-tank company constituted by 12 Reşiţa guns model 1943 of 75 mm.

- A Company of engineers.

- An Antiaircraft Company constituted by hotchkiss guns model 1939 of 25 mm.

- A service company.

- A communications platoon.

This Armored Group of the 4th Romanian Army did not have a long existence either since after participating in some combats in the northwest of Transylvania and in Hungarian territory until the Tisza River, it was dissolved at the beginning of November of 1944. In their confrontations, it is stated that at least 10 TACAM R-2 were lost to the enemies.

As far as the end of 1944, only the 2nd Tank Regiment remained active as an armored unit, which was constituted by:

- 1st tank battalion: with a tank company with 8 T-4 and a company of assault guns with 13 TA.

- 2nd Battalion of tanks (light): with two Tank Companies with 28 R-35 and R-35/45, a Tank Company T-38 with 9 units and a TACAM Battery with 5 TACAM R-2.

- A group of reconnaissance tanks: with 2 R-2.

- An anti-aircraft battery: equipped with 4 anti-aircraft guns Gustloff model 1938 of 20 mm.

- A Recognition Company: endowed with 8 AB and 5 TB.

- A command company.

- A radio communications platoon.

- A cable communications squad.

- A squad of engineers.

Many of the men who were integrated into the 2nd Battle Tank Regiment had served in the recently dissolved 1st Tank of Combat Tanks, among which was the Romanian Ion S Dumitru.

The defensive structure of the Axis in the southern zone of Hungary fell to the Army Group South under the command of General Johannes Friessner. This had the Second Hungarian Army (under the command of General Jeno Major) where the 2nd Magyar Armored Division, the III Hungarian Army (commanded by General József Heszlény) where the 1st Hungarian Armored Division and the 6th German Army were framed (commanded by General Maximiliam Fretter-Pico). The defending troops had about 80000 men (50000 Magyars and 30000 Germans), 300 armored, 3,500 guns and about 500 aircraft.

In front of them, the Soviets and Romanians of the 2nd Ukrainian Front presented some 260000 men (200000 Soviet and 60000 Romanian), 825 armored, more than 10000 guns and about 1,000 aircraft. These were framed in 10 armies (8 Soviet and 2 Romanian): VII Army of the Guard, VI Armored Army of the Guard, XVII, XL and LIII Armies, the Mechanized Cavalry Groups "Pliyev" and "Gorshkov", reserve troops ; as well as the I and IV Romanian Armies, with the support of the Romanian armored formation.

CHAPTER IX

1945. Fight Until The End And Annihilation

According to Pusca, Nitu, and Axworthy, the 2nd Romanian Tank Regiment would have the opportunity to participate for a few months in the fighting against its former German and Hungarian allies, although not as an independent unit. The Soviets were not willing to allow the Romanians any initiative in the combats to come. So that the Romanian 2nd Tank Regiment would be assigned to the Soviet 27th Guard Armored Corps in March 1945, being under the command of this.

At the beginning of the year 1945, the German-Hungarian troops in former Czechoslovakia and in Hungary were facing a great Soviet offensive that made them retreat day after day towards the interior of the Reich. It was at this time that the Soviet High Command finally decided to incorporate the Romanian armored unit into the fighting.

The first destination of his journey against the Axis was Slovakia, where the 2nd Romanian Tank Regiment was sent in February 1945, to be later sent to the front line and assigned to the 27th Armored Corps of the Soviet Guard in the month of March. Coincidentally, this Soviet unit had been the rival of the "Romania Mare" Division 1st Tank Regiment in the clashes in August 1944; and now they were his allies.

The 2nd Battle Tank Regiment was supplied by the Soviets between the months of February and May 1945 with various armored vehicles captured from the Germans (mainly Pz.IV and StuG) with the idea of maintaining combat capability despite the losses suffered. Despite this, the most modern and powerful battle tank of the Romanians was the Pz.IV (T-4) with the StuG III tank destroyer (TA), being the other armored vehicles completely obsolete to face the Pz.IV, Panther, and Tiger of the Germans.

Framed in the Soviet offensive by the capture of Bratislava (capital of Slovakia) and Brno (capital of Moravia) that took place between March 25 and May 5, 1945, with the troops of the 2nd Ukrainian Front commanded by Marshal Malinovsky, the Romanian armored troops continued its participation in the war. We recall that the 1st and 4th Romanian Armies (this one with armored vehicles too) were integrated into the 53rd and 40th Soviet Armies respectively, also belonging to the 2nd Ukrainian Front.

On Sunday, March 25, the 2nd Tank Regiment was ordered to go to the front line, being received by enemy artillery fire. The Romanian armor was prepared to take positions to cross the river Hron, which could be done without great difficulty because it was not very wide. On March 26, the Romanian 2nd Tank Regiment had 9 T-4s, 14 TAs, 9 T-38s, 28 R-35s and R-35/45s, 5 TACAM R-2s and 2 R-2s.

In the early hours of the 26th, the crossing of the river began, with the intervention of the Romanians in Slovak lands. The orders of the Romanian Regiment were to attack in the sector of the towns of Dol-Besa and Dol Pial (Besa and Dolny Pial) with the 2nd Tank Regiment 1st Battalion commanded by Major Cociu and with the 2nd Tank Regiment 2nd Battalion too. After the armored Romanian formation, the Soviet infantry (like the 93rd Rifle Division) followed closely to take possession of the territories "liberated" by the Romanians. Among the Romanian armor, as we have said, there was the obsolete Renault R-35, which showed its shortcomings in combat. One of these tanks of French origin was directed by the Cpt. Arcadie Duceac, who commanded the 2nd Tank Regiment 2nd Battalion 1st Company. The unit led by Duceac took part in the operations to take the town of Dol Pial with the support of the 43rd Rifle Regiment (belonging to the 93rd Rifle Division); achieving the capture of the city. Shortly after, they also managed to stop a German counterattack that had artillery support. The results on March 26, was positive at the tactical level due to the achievement of the objectives set, but on a material and human level, several tanks and several men were lost.

Among the tank commanders that started this offensive on the 26th, there was the ace Slt. Ion S Dumitru, who continued to increase the number of victims in front of the fire of his T-4 gun (formerly the Soviets and now the victims where their former allies: the Germans). After crossing the river, Dumitru and his platoon of T-4 tanks advanced into the enemy lines, destroying at least 6 anti-tank guns along with their towing vehicles. Later, they destroyed a 150mm howitzer to subsequently capture the remains of the 150mm howitzer battery. The tank squad led by the Slt. Ion S Dumitru continued their advance until they came across a Tiger tank platoon, which forced them to stop. Dumitru, knowing his inferiority in front of that German tank model, looked for a way to attack them by the flanks until they made the position that the Tiger occupy untenable until finally, the Germans had to retreat.

The German resistance during this day was very intense, which caused numerous casualties in the 2nd Regiment (at least in the 1st Battalion 1 NCO and three dead soldiers plus 5 missing, and in the 2nd Battalion four officers and four dead soldiers).

As it can be seen, the Romanian casualties, both humans, and vehicles on the first day of the offensive, were important (taking into account the small size of the 2nd Tank Regiment and the absolute dependence on the Soviets for any type of repairs or replacement for their losses in combat).

On the 27th the town of Dol Pial had been completely cleared of enemies, being the launching base of a new Romanian advance at sunset that day. On this occasion, the Romanian armored vehicles headed towards the towns of Tegla (Tehla) and Melek.

The Romanian advance continued on the 28th, after crossing the river by the bridge in the town of Martinova. From there the Regiment progressed to locations such as Gor Siles (Dolny Siles) or Mal-Chetin. In this last locality, the Dumitru´s squad faced against a German armored formation, to which at least they managed to destroy 1 Pz.IV, 1 StuG, 1 SPW 250 and 2 anti-tank guns with their towing vehicles. Thanks to this courageous action of Dumitru´s armored vehicles, the Germans decided to retreat, leaving the town in the hands of the Soviet troops that followed the armored Romanian unit.

The advance of the Romanian armor supported by the Soviet infantry continued inexorably. On March 29 they managed to cross the Nitra River through Surami (Surany), and they continued advancing towards Branci (Branc), where they stopped to reorganize. From there they advanced the next day towards Pania (Pana), with little resistance from the Germans.

The next day, March 31st, the Germans reappeared with tenacious resistance thanks to the use of a Tiger tank squad, another Ferdinand tank destroyer platoon and a Pz. IV tank company (quite possibly the latter could be Hungarians). Despite the strong German-Hungarian resistance, this could fall apart thanks to the use of intense artillery fire that managed to knock out the Ferdinad tank and damage 2 Tigers. Faced with this answer from the Soviets, the defenders decided to retreat (taking with them the two damaged Tigers). In this moment of confusion, Ion S Dumitru and his T-4, went at full speed against the Hungarian Pz.IVs who were unprotected because the Tiger was gone, succeeding in destroying two of them and damaging two others.

On the same day, the population of Ireg was also occupied by the Romanians using 2 Sdkfz 251 and men belonging to the 141st Soviet Rifle Division. The German answer to this attack was an intense artillery fire that could be dislodged neither Romanians nor Soviets from Ireg.

In the last hours of March 31 and the dawn of April 1, the Romanian 2nd Tank Regiment in conjunction with the Soviet infantry launched a night assault against the population controlled by the Germans on the heights close to Bratislava (the defense of the city of Bratislava was entrusted to units of the 6th German Army and the 3rd Hungarian Army). At first, the surprise worked thanks to the darkness and especially to the action of the T-4 belonging to the 1st Battalion that caused the initial withdrawal of the defenders, but the consequent German artillery support paralyzed the Romanians and Soviets. It was the slt. Ion S Dumitru who managed to stop the artillery fire by destroying the church tower where possibly the observer who directed the firing of the German artillery was. In spite of it, the tenacious German resistance motivated that the clashes lasted until the dawn, finalizing with the victory of Rumanian and Soviet troops. In this confrontation at least were destroyed one German Pz.IV and six SPW 250.

Once the starting positions for the assault on Bratislava were taken, it started. On April 2, the Romanian 2nd Tank Regiment approached the Slovak capital through the town of Pania (Pana), where they regrouped, waiting to continue the progress the next day. That night, they were subjected to the bombs of several night bombers (called "Mos Costica" by the Romanians), without causing significant damage.

On April 3, Bratislava fell into the hands of Soviet troops. The Romanian 2nd Tank Regiment didn't have the opportunity during the assault on the city to face other German armored units, only with infantry and some artillery pieces.

At dusk (around 5:00 pm), an armored vehicle SPW (Sdkfz 251) was sent to the city commanded by second lieutenant Grigore Dobos to verify the situation of the city and if the defenders had been completely eliminated; as it would be confirmed. The conquest of the city had not caused significant losses to the Romanian armored unit, which set out to reorganize itself for the next day to continue its advance through Slovak lands.

At dawn on day 4, the 2nd Tank Regiment after a short break and pass through Bratislava (as a curiosity the Romanian unit still had two old R-2 in service), headed towards the Morava River, which they had planned to traverse in a ship. But the first attempt of crossing carried out by the vehicles of the 1st Battalion was prevented by the bombing of enemy planes.

It was necessary to wait until April 5 for the Romanian unit to cross the Morava and continue its progress through enemy territory. In this advance, the 7 battle tanks (T-4) in combat service conditions from the 1st Battalion along with three TAs, were under the command of slt. Ion S Dumitru; who was entrusted with the capture of Devinska. The Romanian-Soviet attack was preceded by the destructive use of Katyusha rockets that forced the German defenders to take new positions, although always waiting for ambushes upon the arrival of the Romanian tanks. What continued was the clash for an hour and a half of a small German armored group against the Detachment led by Dumitru. The best positioning of the Romanian armor allowed the Germans to retreat, leaving behind 3 SPWs and 9 tanks and StuG IIIs, which were destroyed. Again the ability of Dumitru to lead their armor allowed settling this clash against the Germans with a brilliant victory.

On the 6th and 7th, after a short break, the 2nd Romanian Tank Regiment marked as a new objective in its journey to the German Reich, in particular to Austria (framed within the Soviet offensive by Vienna that took place between March 16and April 15, 1945). The main contact with the enemy during these days consisted of the action of the German aviation which tried unsuccessfully to destroy the Romanian armor. Both the Soviets and their Romanian allies were rushing towards Vienna, to take the imperial city, one of the main capitals of the German Reich.

At dawn on the 8th, the German resistance grew when stepping on the floor of the Reich. Specifically, around 5.00 am the Romanian 2nd Tank Regiment was positioned in the foothills of a forest near the town of Hohenruppersdorf, where some German troops were preparing to defend their national territory. Again and as usual, the assault began with the intense fire of the Soviet artillery and the Katyushas, who struck the German defenses in that locality at 8.30 am. Already with the German defenders very depleted, the T-4s from the 1st Battalion (commanded by Dumitru) went towards the foothills of Hohenruppersdorf, without a great resistance of the enemies. On the other hand, the remains of the armored of the Regiment in union with its allies from 27th Soviet Armored Brigade in its advance received the welcome with a heavy enemy fire. At the end of the day, the town was controlled by the Germans and the Romanian-Soviets had taken positions in the proximity of Hohenruppersdorf.

During April 9th, some German attacks were repelled, without motivating any Romanian-Soviet withdrawal. From their positions, on April 10th, the Romanians could see the arrival of some German armored vehicles to reinforce the town. Before the accumulation of German troops in Hohenruppersdorf, the Soviet High Command decided to launch a new attack against the town, which took place on April 11th. The defender resistance was bitter, managing to make some counterattacks with the Pz.IV that had accumulated in the town. But the Soviets push supported by the Romanian tanks, allowed at the end of the day to occupy practically the whole town and withstand the Germans (according to some source, the two R-2 tanks belonging to Romanian 2nd Tank Regiment, had to get knocked out in these clashes against the Germans).

Once the victory was achieved, the Soviets understood how dangerous it could be to spend the night in the town, due to the proximity of the Germans. Despite this, it was decided to leave a garrison at Hohenruppersdorf which consisted of a small detachment (specifically Dumitru with two T-4s, as well as an infantry platoon and a Soviet anti-tank gun battery) watching the town during that night.

As the Soviets supposed the German resistance had not ended, so at dawn on April 12th, they launched a surprise counterattack against Hohenruppersdorf. The Germans at 4:00 am sent 4 SPWs to study the area, which surprised the Soviet infants by forcing them to retreat. In the face of such an emergency, Dumitru had to organize the defense of the population with his two T-4s. After locating the four German armors, managed to take them and destroy the first of them, allowing the Soviet antitank battery to destroy two other armors, making one of them escape unharmed.

It was not long before the bulk of the mixed German force with infantry and several armored vehicles (apparently between them were Hungarian troops belonging to the 25th SS Division "Hunyadi" and the 26th SS Division "Hungaria") were again launched against Hohenruppersdorf, only an hour later, Dumitru could appreciate as a small armored formation composed of 4 Pz.IVs and 4 SPWs entered the town again. Despite their numerical inferiority, the two Romanian T-4s and the Soviet antitank managed to give the best of themselves. A Pz.IV fell under the fire of the Soviets while the other 3 Pz.IVs continued their advance without noticing that Dumitru's own T-4 had been positioned behind them. From his ambush position, Dumitru destroyed the Pz.IV that was in the middle. When subjected to the fire of the Romanian tanks and Soviet guns, the crews of the other Pz.IsV surrendered and left their tanks with their arms raised. While this was happening, the other Romanian T-4 in Hohenruppersdorf destroyed 2 SPWs, although without being able to prevent the other 2 SPWs from escaping.

This brilliant defensive action of Dumitru with only two T-4s, the anti-tank battery and the Soviet infantry squad, allowed to bring to light the good work of the Romanian ace that despite the numerical inferiority made his tactical good work prevail. The result was very clear, 2 Pz.IVs and 2 SPWs destroyed, 2 Pz.IVs captured in exchange for no losses in the anti-tank or in the Romanian T-4s (yes suffered some casualties Soviet infants).

At dawn on April 13th, after having stopped the German attack of the previous day, the Soviet-Romanians were again attacked by German artillery fire supported by tactical bombing by Luftwaffe planes, when the Soviet-Romanians were in the process of regrouping. They were joined by some armored Germans who tried to control the town. Despite the first panic moments that caused a slight retreat in the Soviet-Romanians, they finally managed to repel completely the Germans from Hohenruppersdorf, who finally fled in the direction of Sric (Schrick).

The final result after the combats by Hohenruppersdorf both in the Romanian 2nd Tank Regiment and in the unit to which it was attached (the 27th Guard Armored Corp) was very negative, since they had suffered many casualties considering that they had been fighting for a small town in the Reich that the Germans had defended whatever the cost may be.

In the Romanian unit, there were at least 5 tanks damaged, 10 dead and several injured; a force restructuration was necessary; so that the Romanian Regiment was outspread northwest of Hohenruppersdorf and proceeded to reorganize, specifically in Nexing. Due to the losses suffered, it was decided that the 1st Tank Battalion 1st Tank Company would assume the role of Mixed Company that would group the best-armored vehicles available to the 2nd Regiment.

The slt. Dumitru who was appointed the officer in command of the 1st Tank Battalion 1st Tank Company immediately received orders to direct an attack towards Sric (where the Germans had become strong after their withdrawal from Hohenruppersdorf) on April 14th. The armored group that he commanded was composed of 6 T-4s, 3 TAs, 2 R-2s (it´s possible that these 2 tanks were out of service after the clashes for Hohenruppersdorf), 5 TACAM and 3 other armored vehicles (without specifying which type they were).

Dumitru´s commanding did not last long, since, in their attack on April 14th, they faced 3 German Panthers who attacked them by surprise from a flank, causing the Romanian unit to lose 2 T-4s and 1 TACAM, apart from leaving another T-4 out of combat. This last T-4 was commanded by the stl. Dumitru, who suffered significant injuries that caused him to be removed from his duty. The position that Dumitru vacated, was occupied by Cpt. Arcadie Duceac (remember that he was the previous commander of the 2nd Tank Regiment 2nd Battalion 1st Company on April 17th). During just over 20 fighting days, Duceac demonstrated his great courage and ability to make the most of obsolete armored vehicles. According to experts in the matter, Dumitru during the 5 days he fought in August 1944 against the Soviets and the 20 days in 1945 in which he fought alongside the Soviets, managed to destroy 5 tanks and 3 or 4 armored vehicles (from 39 tanks and 13 armored vehicles that managed to destroy the unit that Dumitru commanded). For these merits acquired in combat, he received the highest Romanian decoration in wartime, the 3rd class Ordinul Mihai Viteazul with swords.

When taking the command of the Mixed Company, this was ready for combat with 1 T-4 platoon, 1 TA platoon, and 1 R-35 platoon. Although the war was almost finalized, with the Germans in withdrawal on all fronts, there was still to give the final blow of grace to the Germans. So the Soviets called for a new effort to the Romanian armored unit, which consisted of the capture of the Austrian towns of Wilfersdorf and Aspern. The first one was taken by the unit of Cpt.Duceac on April 18th and the second on April 19th; and in both cases the Romanians were supported by the 4th Soviet Rifle Division.

On April 19th, around 6 p.m. a mixed German formation composed of several tanks and infantry attacked the Duceac Mixed Company. With great combat spirit, Duceac tanks managed to repel first and then push back the enemy, but not before having destroyed at least 2 tanks, 1 SPW, 2 anti-tank guns and 12 machine guns. As it is logical to suppose, they were mainly the T-4 belonging to the platoon commanded by the slt. Iosif Forgaci, the cause of most of the German casualties.

The German withdrawal took place towards Eibenstahl, where they tried to reorganize, although they could not achieve it since the Romanian Mixed Company and the remains of the 2nd Tank Regiment immediately went to the aforementioned town with the intention of destroying the remains of the German combat formation. But the Germans became strong and managed to counterattack the Romanians, causing the destruction of one of the venerable R-2 still had the Romanians in service; while for its part the Romanians managed to damage two tanks and two German SPWs. The German resistance in Eibenstahl was so obstinate that the 2nd Romanian Regiment received orders to outflank the town, a fact that was achieved without major difficulties.

The 2nd Romanian Tank Regiment combats in Austria came to an end when the 27th Guard Armored Corp was again assigned to Czechoslovakia. For its new deployment, the Romanian armored unit was reinforced with 2 obsolete R-35s. The transfer of the 2nd Romanian Tank Regiment was made from the north-eastern Austrian region to the south of Czechoslovakia, with the city of Brno as the reference address. We have evidence of war activity of the 2nd Romanian Tank Regiment already in the Czechoslovak territory around 25-30 of April of 1945. On April 26th at around 4.00 am, the Romanian unit crossed the Morava River towards Musov (Na Muslove) to immediately see its advance slowed down by the fire of German tanks (Tigers?) That destroyed a T-4 at sunset on the same day. The next day around 10.00 am, there was a German counterattack that pushed back the Soviet infantry at first and then with the help of the Romanian armor to repel the Germans. But the pressure continued on the Soviet-Romanian formation that had taken defensive positions in Musov since they were subjected to artillery fire that tried to annihilate them. On April 28th and until April 30th the German artillery fire persisted over Soviets and Romanians in Musov, which, although they were violently answered by the latter, failed to completely clear the road to Brno during those days.

These battles lasted until April 30, and the Mixed Company commanded by the Cpt.Duceac in support of the 409th Guard Division had some hard confrontations against a mixed German group composed of several Panther tanks and infantry in the area that was between the towns of Musov and Nova Ves. After these days with several clashes on the road that led to the city of Brno (which had been taken by Soviet forces on April 26th), the Soviet-Romanian forces achieved victory, but the damage suffered by the Romanians (remember that any repair of their damaged vehicles or the incoming of new vehicles to replace casualties, was subject to a rigorous control by the Soviets, which led into the practical annihilation of the 2nd Tank Regiment after those combats, since during this period they were only reinforced with 1 Pz.IV yielded by the Soviets and 2 Pz.IVs captured by the Romanians during the combats) made them less and less useful to carry out any combat activity. But the Soviets weren't ready to give the old German allies some rest (except for the celebration that the Romanians shared with the soldiers of the 27th Guard Armored Corp during May 1). Despite the obvious defeat of the Germans, they did not want to be captured by the Soviets and tried to stop the Russian advance as it was. In fact, on May 3rd the Germans made a small counter-attack in the Romanian deployment zone, although it was repelled without further consequences; for May 4 and May 5 began to gather artillery and Katiushas in large numbers (according to sources, the number of 200 artillery guns of several types and caliber was reached)trying to unleash a big blow to the Germans.

On May 7th at 5.30 am, the Soviet artillery began to destroy the German defensive lines. The rain of fire lasted two hours and left the German troops quite depleted. That was the moment in which the Soviet High Command ordered the Romanian armored unit that with just a few T-4s and R-35s still in service attack on May 7th near Pasohlavki. This Soviet-Romanian attack was part of the offensive towards Prague and allowed at least 7 German possessed towns to be captured on May 7th. Fortunately for the Romanians, they did not have to regret the loss of any more tanks. The next day, on May 8th, the persecution of the retreating Germans continued, they barely offered resistance. For this reason, the Romanian 2nd Tank Regiment advanced up to 70 kilometers and reached Znaim (Znajmo), where they stopped their march to continue it the next day. But at dawn on May 9th, they received the news that Germany had surrendered unconditionally and that the peace had reached Europe. Although in fact there were still some resistance pockets in wooded areas with mainly SS troops who refused to accept to surrender and who were going to be destroyed. So that although the War was over, the remains of the 2nd Tank Regiment were sent to Telci (Telc).

After the last combat day maintained by the remains of the 2nd Tank Regiment, practically the Unit was almost out of combat because of the damage suffered; so the end of the fighting capacity of the Romanian armored group coincided with the end of hostilities in Europe after the German surrender.

During the battles between February and May 1945, the Romanian 2nd Tank Regiment was first in Czechoslovakia, then in Austria and finally again in Czechoslovakia, the Romanian group fought almost continuously demonstrating high fighting spirit. This fact can be confirmed by the fact that they were mentioned by the Soviet High Command four times for their courageous actions in combat. Although in the first moments the Romanian 2nd Tank Regiment was not a powerfully armored formation (remember that only the T-4s and TAs were at an acceptable skill to face the German armor, the other armored vehicles being quite obsolete by 1945), and after the continuous combats to which the Soviet High Command ordered them to take part became in the first days of May in a Unit with very little fighting capacity. Despite this, they managed to destroy in his various clashes again the enemies, at least 9 Pz.IVs, 6 Pz Vs (Panther) and 6 Pz.VIs (Tiger).

In just a couple of months of fighting the casualties reached 93% of the armored vehicles (only one T-4 survived the fighting in service conditions). Having always demonstrated great value in the combat line, the Soviets did not want to allow the Romanian 2nd Tank Regiment to continue to exist after the end of World War II, forcing the Romanians to hand over the few armored vehicles that were still in service and later they dissolved the Romanian 2nd Tank Regiment. A hard time began to fall on Romania.

Despite the dissolution of the Romanian 2nd Tank Regiment, the Soviets already had in mind the creation of a new Romanian armored force, in which many Romanian prisoners of war would be an important role. The new unit was constituted on

June 15 and for its talent, the armored material that the Soviets offered to Romania for the new armored formation, was not new material or from the Soviet manufacture but captured from the Germans during the war conflict. So they were supplied with several typed of armored vehicles like Pz.IV, Pz.V Panther Ausf A, Pz.V Panther Ausf D, Pz.V Panther Ausf G, StuG III Ausf G, JgPz.IV/70 and a Hummel.

Reckoning After The War

At the end of the war, Romania had to face painful and harsh circumstances. The Romanian Army was dismantled in large part due to the distrust they generated in Moscow. This fact was very evident when many Romanian soldiers who had fought against the USSR were interned in prison camps. The Romanian troops that the Soviet Union allowed continuing existing were pro-communist troops that collaborated without any problem with the directives that departed from Moscow or were under strict surveillance so that they could not provoke any kind of military uprising. Also, many of the militaries were stigmatized and were not allowed to ascend within the military career, as in the case of the Ion Dumitru, who despite continuing in the Army as a tank instructor until 1953, was not promoted despite his merits in combat.

It was not only the Army that suffered the consequences of the change of Romanian side because the people were the other great victim. After the end of the war, Romania had the status of an occupied country and the pro-communists were seizing power. As early as 1946, after an inconclusive election, the first steps were taken. In 1947 the monarchy was abolished and finally the Republic was proclaimed on December 31, 1947. After that, and without opposition, the communist Government installed itself in power until 1989.

ANNEXES

Annex 1: Insignias Of The Romanian Armored Forces

The insignias used by the Romanian armored forces varied throughout the world conflict. They were mainly three, the types of badges used: a tricolor circle with the national colors, the Michael Cross and a red star on a white circle.

At the beginning of the World War II, Romania, which was not yet a belligerent country, used the same insignia on its armored vehicles as on its air forces. This consisted of a circle with the three colors of the Romanian national flag: red (outside ring) - yellow (middle ring) - blue (an inner disc). Its main use was until June 1941, although it is true that there are images in which this badge coexisted with the Michael Cross.

Until September 1940 was painted in the turrets of both R-1 and R-2 tanks, the Royal crest badge that represented the king Carol´s II cypher surrounded by two laurel leaves branches with a royal crown above (because Carol´s abdication the II was removed). During the war the badge was used with a darker shade of paint that made it a low visibility badge.

After the beginning of the war and the fights of Romania in the Eastern Front, it begins to use a new badge: the Michael Cross. As it happened in other Axis countries, the national badge corresponded to crosses (Germany, Hungary or Finland for example) so this symbol was chosen. This cross was the royal seal of Michael I and its official denomination was "Cifra Regala a Regelui Mihai 1 al Romanilor". It consisted of a yellow cross bounded by 4 "M" in blue and the tricolor shield in the center; although there were several models of it. Its use was between June of 1941 and August of 1944. This badge was very visible from long distances because of its brightness and contrast, so much that it turned out to be an easy target, reason why it was preferred to leave a simplified cross (to the extend of becoming just the outline of the cross in black or white without any filling other than the color of the tank) on the sides of the hull tank. Sometimes as in the R-35s was painted in white in the right side of the rear part of the hull. Furthermore, the Cross with the three national colors (as in the Royal Romanian Air Force) was used on the engine (to improve aerial reconnaissance). Also, as we have said, it was combined with the tricolor circular badge on top of the turret.

In spite of this distribution of badges, in many occasions the Michael Cross was not used continuously since 1943.

Although the Unit badges were not officially issued, sometime they were allowed in order to raise the unit "esprit du corps". The cavalry badge (although it was only seen at some subunits of the cavalry moto-mechanized troops) was a drawing of Saint George killing a dragon in white. It was painted on the turret of the cavalry vehicles as AH-IV tanks.

After the Romania change of side in August of 1944 (in the called Western campaign), the few armored forces that remained in service did it mainly close to the Soviets, so the previous markings were removed because were similar to the German cross. In this period two badges coexisted. On the one hand, since September 1944, the use of the tricolor circular badge was reinstated (in spring 1945 a rectangle with three national colors diagonally placed was adopted). On the other hand and until the end of the war, the Romanian armored vehicles belonging to the 2nd Tank Regiment that fought shoulder to shoulder with the Soviet troops carried a new insignia consisting of a five pointed red star on a circular white background (in some pictures is seen as a khaki star).

Annex 2: Armored Vehicles Of The Romanian Army

The Armored Romanian Forces, as we have observed through the text, were unable to confront the powerful Soviet enemy as an equal during all phases of the World War. In spite of this, it is worth mentioning the meritorious attempt by the Romanian Government to obtain an armored force that at least partially was based in the native production, although the materials were from vehicles captured from the Soviets. While it is true that the course of the war prevented the development of the latest Romanian designs, such as the Mareşal tank-hunter, that should have entered the active service would very possibly have been in conditions of equality or even superiority against their Soviet opponents. The Romanian's need finally allowed Germany to bring various types of armor to Hungary, among which it is worth noting the main "battle horses" of the German Army: the StuG III and the Panzerkampfwagen IV, although in quantities greater than the number of crews prepared to use them. This situation motivated, as we narrated in the text, that a good number of StuG III and the Romanian-owned Panzerkampfwagen IV were manned by Germans.

In this section we will make a brief review of the most significant armored vehicles of different characteristics that, to a greater or lesser extent, formed part of the Romanian Army during the second world conflict, with special emphasis on the various hybrid tank-hunters of Romanian manufacture. The works of Pusca, Nitu, and Axworthy have been important sources to know more about the matter.

Foreign Armored Vehicles In The First Years Of The War

1) FT

The FT-17 was a tank of French origin that can be considered as the first modern battle tank, with a hull complemented by a manual 360 degree turret with 37 mm gun or an 8 mm machine gun. We can confirm its worth by the fact that it was in service in the French Army from the World War I to the beginning of the World War II. This armored came to the Romanian arsenal in 1919 thanks to a Franco-Romanian pact for which they were acquired 76 FT-17 (48 with 37mm Puteaux gun and 28 armed with an 8mm Hotchkiss machine gun), being called FT in Romania. With them the 1st Romanian Tank Regiment was established in the same year. This tank began to be obsolete in the period between wars, but at the beginning of World War II, it was below in performance of any of the armored vehicles that were manufactured in Europe. To try to solve this problem in part, they were modernized until 1939 by the Leonida workshops and the Army arsenal in Bucharest.

At the start of World War II, the FT-17s were grouped in the FT Tank Battalion and were never sent to the front lines for obvious reasons. They were used in internal security missions in industrial zones and urban centers in Romania like in Bucharest, Ploieşti, Sibiu or Reşiţa). They were also used to train new tank crews. His only intervention during the war was the one that they had after the Romania changed of side in 1944 (August 23) when they faced German troops, acting with success. Only a few months later, in February 1945, all the Romanian FT minus one were seized by the Soviets. The only one that remained in Romania, remains exposed in the Military Museum of Bucharest.

	Nationality	Crew	Weight (ton)	Main weapon (mm)	Speed km/h	Main armor (mm)
FT	France	2	6.5	37 mm	7.72	22
r-1	Czechoslovakia	2	3.5	7.92 mm	45	12

2) R-1

The AH-IV was a Czechoslovak tank manufactured by the Českomoravská Kolben-Daněk (CKD). It had a weight of about 3.5 tons, so it can also be classified as a light tank (according to the pre-war guns). As it happened with a large part of the armored vehicles manufactured by Czechoslovakia, it was a versatile vehicle with adequate performance. It was armed with a 7.92 mm ZB-37 heavy machine gun, as well as with a 7.92 mm ZB-30 light machine gun also. It reached a speed of 45 km/h by road and 20 km/h cross-country thanks to a Prague engine RHR V6 60 hp. Its main problem lays in the thinness of its armor, which was only 15 mm in its front area (in units purchased by Romania would be only 12 mm).

On April 1st, 1936 the Romanian Army accepted the AH-IV tank as appropriate and on August 1st of the same year made an order to the CKD of 36 units. According to another source, although its veracity was not confirmed and less credible, it was up to 75 copies of the R-1 that Romania received?. Although to satisfy the Romanians, several modifications had to be made, leading to them being called R-1 in Romania. The R-1 differed from the AH-IV in that they had no dome for the commander, the armor was smaller, the engine was 50 hp (or at least the original engines were modified to only reach 50 hp instead of 60 hp, with the intention of increasing its operating time). On the positive side, the R-1 was more agile, faster and with greater autonomy than the original AH-IV (reaching up to 160 kilometers).

The first R-1 tanks arrived in Romania at the beginning of 1937, although the total number of units was completed in April 1938. However it was not until August 1938 that the R-1 was finally incorporated into its military units. .

The use of the tanks in the Romanian Army proved its worth, consequently in 1939 before the impossibility of obtaining enough tanks from France, Romania opted to negotiate with Czechoslovakia to construct 380 AH-IV under license of the Malaxa company. These tanks would be renamed R-1-a and should reinforce the armored component of the Romanian Army.

But the events that were taking place in Europe motivated that this manufacturing license was never fulfilled. Only one copy of the R-1-a was built and had a dome for the tank commander; being apparently the prototype that the CKD presented to the Romanians for the production of the tank in Romania.

The R-1 tanks were incorporated into the Cavalry Brigades reconnaissance squads (specifically the 1st, 5th, 6th, 7th, 8th and 9th); that since March 25, 1942 were re-designated as Cavalry Divisions. The number of R-1 in each squadron was variable although it ranged from 4 to 6 units (the 1st, 7th and 9th Cavalry Brigades received 4, and the 5th, 6th and 8th received 6); with two platoons composed of two or three tanks in each Cavalry Brigade.

They were very useful in tasks of reconnaissance in combat, although its scarce shielding turned out to be an important inconvenience. The 18 R-1 that were in the Romanian Cavalry Corps in the initial phases of Operation Barbarossa were only used until October 1st. Later between 1941 and 1942 they participated in combats in the south of the Ukraine and in the Caucasus integrated in the Cavalry Corps (with the 5ª, 6ª and 8ª Cavalry Brigades). They also participated in the combats destined to capture Odessa, also within the cavalry units.

The four R-1 tanks that were available to the 1st Cavalry Division Mechanized Squadron during "Operation Uranus" (when they were surrounded by the Soviet Army in November 1942), were burned before delivering them to the enemy, as they did not have fuel for them. On the other hand, there were 5 R-1s of the 5th and 8th Cavalry Divisions that were also lost during the Romanian withdrawal in "Operation Uranus" and subsequent intervention in "Operation Wintergewitter" (Winter Storm) that would consist of an attack by the Army Group Don in front of the river Chir to try to reach Stalingrad and break the siege to which the city was subjected by the Soviets.

On the other hand, some of the Romanian R-1s that were on the Kuban bridge-head were lost to enemy fire, only 2 of them being repatriated to Romania in the spring of 1943.

The few surviving R-1 tanks, which participated in their last battle with the Axis during the battle for Stalingrad in the Romanian sectors or in the Kuban and Crimea, were removed from active duty in combat to be used solely for training tasks in the Cavalry Training Center. On August 30, 1943 there were 13 R-1s in operation assigned to the Cavalry Training Center, which increased by one more R-1 later.

There is no evidence that the R-1 participated in the fighting of August 1944 against the Soviets, although after the Romania change of side, some R-1 were incorporated into the 2nd Tank Regiment that fought with the Soviets against Hungarians and Germans. Between March 26, 1945 (which is when they reached the battle front) and April 24, 1945, the number of R-1 Regiment fell to 1, to subsequently disappear from the inventory of vehicles in service in the Regiment.

3) R-2

This Czechoslovak origin armored vehicle made by the leading company Škoda represented the first modern tank that was available to the Romanian Army. Its arrival in the country was motivated by the plan of renewal of the Romanian armed forces in 1935. After studying various candidates, the chosen one was the Czechoslovak light tank LT-35 (also known in its manufacturing line as the Š-IIa-R) of 10.5 tons, of which an order of 126 units was made on August 14th, 1936.

The first 15 copies were sent to Romania between April and May 1937, being able to take part in a parade of the Romanian Armed Forces. These first copies rented by Czechoslovakia were useful for the Romanians to begin to appreciate the possibilities of the new tank, but also the problems they had when being used. They were tested until July 1938 when on the 28th in the same month they were returned to the Škoda factory to recondition them and make a series of modifications, which would determine that the tank would be renamed R-2 instead of LT-35. During this period of preparation of the R-2, Romania demanded that the initial tests to determine all the improvements that would be implemented in the LT-35 were carried out in Romania, in response Škoda agreed and sent 3 copies on July 12th, 1938 to Romania to be tested in Baragan, near Suditi. After the good results obtained, Romania finally approved the design of the R-2 on August 23rd.

The main differences between the R-2 and the LT-35 consisted of slight modifications in the turret and the hull of the tank (although without affecting the thickness of the armor that was 25 mm in the front area and 16 mm in the sides). It mounted the same LT-35 engine, the Škoda T-11/0 118 hp, which allowed it to reach speeds of up to 35 km/h. And as main armament had a 37 mm gun and two 7.92mm ZB-53 machine guns.

This process of modifying the LT-35 until converting it into R-2 evidently brought with it a significant delay in the delivery of the tank to Romania. The problems that already hindered manufacturing of the LT-35, together with some possibly non-essential modifications made it necessary to wait until 1939 for the tank to finally reach the Romanian Army.

Although as we said, the tank in Romanian version was the R-2, there was also another model of R-2 with new modifications, the R-2c (its main difference with the initial model being: the armor was cemented giving it greater strength and a different appearance in the back of the turret contour and the tank hull). Virtually among all the R-2 that arrived in Romania, half corresponded to each version.

Also the convulsive situation in central Europe in 1938 and 1939 caused the Romanian request to be further delayed. The reason was that the 27 tanks completed at the Škoda factory were requisitioned in Czechoslovakia in the face of the danger that was looming over the country (although they were finally sent to Romania after the Munich Agreement). It was not until October 1938 that the Romanian order was resumed, then stopped again due to the border conflict with Hungary. Finally, on February 22, 1939, 32 copies of the R-2 left Pilsen in the direction of Romania. The first order of 126 tanks was delivered in 1939, but a second order of 382 new tanks was not finally accomplished because Germany (already controlling the Czechoslovak armament industry) refused to sell them.

As we discussed in the text, the R-2 and R-2c formed the core of the 1st Romanian Armored Division 1st Tank Regiment during its intervention in the Soviet Union in the years 1941 and 1942. It can be considered that its behavior in combat was acceptable at first (Barbarrosa, conquest of Chisinau) then decreasing its performance later (in Odessa many of the R-2 caused a loss in the 1st Armored Division 1st Tank Regiment) because it was becoming obsolete quickly before the appearance of antitank weapons and enemy tanks better armed and armored; as well as due to the tactics employed by the Romanians to support the infantry with the tanks that excessively harmed the power and offensive capacity of the R-2s.

After the loss of many R-2s after the capture of Odessa, Germany, at the request of Romania, agreed to deliver 26 Panzerkampfwagen 35(t) from German units to try to compensate somewhat the existing losses in the 1st Romanian Armored Division. This tank was very similar to the R-2 and did not represent an improvement in the quality of the Romanian armored vehicles.

During this period, the Romanians had the opportunity to do some tests with the R-2 when compared to a captured Soviet T-34. The test showed terrible results for the Romanian tank, since the T-34 was practically invulnerable in front of the 37mm gun of the R-2, whereas the R-2 was vulnerable in front of the Soviet tank's gun.

After Odessa, at least 40 R-2s were sent to factories in Pilsen for general review and another 50 to Ploiești (in Romania) for minor repairs. The following highlighted intervention of the R-2 was on the banks of the Don in 1942 integrated into the Romanian 3rd Army (on August 29, 1942 the 1st Armored Division had 109 tanks R-2 against 84 on November 19, since at least 37 tanks rendered useless before reaching their deployment site) as well as in the fighting after the Soviet offensive by Stalingrad. We already know that there the disaster was total, leaving practically annihilated the 1st Armored Division (approximately one third of the lost R-2 were in combat, another third due to mechanical failures and another third to be abandoned due to lack of fuel).

After the disaster of Stalingrad practically the R-2 ceased to be the main tank in Romania (the arrival of the T-4 left them relegated to a second plane within the Romanian armored arsenal). 25 R-2 were in the process of repair at the beginning of the year and only 59 R-2 or Pz.Kpfw. 35 (t) were in operation between April 1 and August 30, 1943. In February 1944 an R-2 company was sent to Transnitria within the "Cantemir" Mixed Armored Group to be retired on March 28 without having participated in any combat. On March 25, 1944, 63 R-2 and Pz.Kpfw 35(t) had already been put into operation.; then the number of available tanks lowered to 44 on July 19, 1944. Due to their obsolescence, the R-2 and Pz.Kpfw. 35 (t) that remained in service were assigned to training tasks with the 1st Armored Training Division.

Although it will be noted in its chapter, 21 R-2 were transformed during 1943-1944 into the TACAM R-2 self-propelled guns when a 76.2 mm Soviet gun was assembled to them.

After the Romania's change of side, some R-2 were used in the area of the oil fields in Ploieşti within the "Popescu" Armored Detachment. In February 1945, Romania still had 5 R-2, although as soon as they tried to be sent to the front, the Soviets prevented it? by confiscating them when they arrived at the front.

The swan song of the R-2 took place when 2 R-2 belonging to the 2nd Tank Regiment in February 1945 participated in the combat actions in Czechoslovakia and Austria. These last two R-2, were definitely lost on April 12 in the fighting that took place in Hohenruppersdorf.

	Nationality	Crew	Weight (ton)	Main weapon (mm)	Speed Km/h	Main armor (mm)
R-2	Czechoslovakia	4	10.5	37	40	25
Malaxa	France	2	2	--	30	7
R-35	France	2	9.8	37	20	40

4) R-35

The second most powerful tank of the Romanian arsenal at the beginning of the World War II was the Renault R-35. This tank of French origin was characterized by its robust shielding (4 cm in the front area), although with its weight of 14 tons it was not fast and the 37 mm gun that it mounted had important deficiencies in front of the rivals that should face in the combats.

The arrival of the R-35 to Romania was originated by the well-known need to improve the military capacity of the country. In the rearmament program that was carried out during the 1930s, Romania intended to obtain a license for the local manufacture of one of the tanks in use in the French Army, the R-35. From December of 1937, the Romanian interest in this tank became patent when Romania began relations with France with such aim. The original idea was to manufacture 200 specimens in Romania, for which, in 1938, the building of a factory for this purpose on Romanian territory was being finalized with France. But the situation in Europe motivated France (traditional friend of Romania) to have problems to meet Romanian demands (in terms of providing the necessary tools to start a factory) when it did not have enough for itself at the possibility of an armed confrontation with Germany, besides being exporting tanks also to Yugoslavia, Poland and Turkey.

Given that production under license was impossible, the Romanians at least did manage to get France to sell 41 R-35s to the Romanian Army. The French tank in Romania was designated as Care of Lupta Tip R-35.

As we have said before, this tank had not excellent performance despite its excellent armoring for the time. Due to its weight, it was extremely slow (20 km/h), had an inadequate suspension, not very powerful gun, the one man turret, a lot of breakdowns and no radio. Although Romania tried to improve some of these problems (for example the suspensions were improved or the French Chatellerault machine gun was changed to a Czechoslovak 7.92 mm ZB-30).

Although at first they were considered suitable tanks for combat, later they had to be relegated to secondary tasks and training.

Although Romania had 41 R-35, this was far from the production of 200 units that had initially thought. Good luck caused that at least in a small percentage this problem was corrected, since the invasion of Poland in September 1939 motivated that many Polish troops fled seeking refuge in neighboring countries. That's how 34 R-35 belonging to the 21st Polish Light Tank Battalion (Batalion Czołgów Lekkich) found asylum in Romania, passing these tanks immediately to join the Romanian R-35s.

So in the last quarter of 1939 the Romanian Army had 75 R-35 (less than the 200 initially desired but enough to create a unit equipped with this model); the so-called 2nd Tank Regiment (established on November 1, 1939) which was extended to two battalions.

The other tank that Romania had a good number of copies of other tank, the R-2, which was much more versatile and displayed better performance than the R-35. For this reason, on June 22, 1941, the R-2 belonging to the 1st Tank Regiment remained as the main tank force in the Romanian 1st Armored Division; while the R-35 belonging to the 2nd Tank Regiment were assigned to the 4th Romanian Army. This determined that its initial main utility was limited to the support of the infantry (as it would do in the capture of Bessarabia and Northern Bucovina or during the combats for the conquest of Odessa with some success) to later be used as stationary artillery (as happened in 1944 in Transnitria).

After the campaign of 1941 in the Soviet Union, it was decided that the 2nd Tank Regiment should be sent to reserve to be used mainly as a training unit located in Transnitria. This period was used for repairs of all kinds in the tank, such as changing chains, tracks, cylinders, etc. With all these small fixes it was possible to increase the operational life period of these tanks.

The obsolescence of the R-35 motivated (as it did with other antiquated armored vehicles of the Romanian arsenal) that the idea of modernizing to arise. The modernization consisted in replacing its original gun with a 45 mm one, giving rise to the so-called Vanatorul de care R-35, which will be discussed in its corresponding section.

Although its use was evidently of little significance during the Soviet offensive of August 1944, the R-35 was again used in combat, although against its previous

German allies. An R-35 Company was integrated into the "Popescu" Armored Detachment that participated in combats for the Ploieşti oil fields at the end of August 1944. Again some R-35 together with the modified R-35/45 were incorporated into the 2nd Tank Regiment. In the subsequent battles in the valley of the Hron River (March 26 and 27, 1945) 8 R-35s were destroyed and 2 damaged. The few R-35s still working were out of service before the end of the war.

5) MALAXA

In the years before the World War II, Romania was trying to acquire an adequate armored force. From as early as 1931, Romania acquired from France some units of the armored artillery tractor Renault Chenillette d'Infanterie Type UE (Renault UE). The vehicle satisfied Romania so that in 1937, it acquired from the French company Renault, the license for the manufacture of 300 units of the armored artillery tractor Renault UE. The start of production of the tractor by the Romanian company Rogifer, formerly Malaxa (from Bucharestk), was in September 1939.

When the production was carried out by the Malaxa, the vehicle ended up receiving the name Senileta Malaxa Tipul UE and in a general way it was known as "Malaxa" simply. Its initial mission should be to pull the anti-tank guns or to transport ammunition and fuel in the various units of motorized cavalry.

For production under license, the Malaxa industry had to receive the pieces from the Renault company, but the situation in France at the beginning of the armed conflict, motivated that in 1941 they stopped sending pieces to Romania. Up to that time, 126 units of Senileta Malaxa Tipul UE had been manufactured in Romania. Some more units of the Renault tractor were later acquired by Romania to Germany (which had them as spoils of war captured in France).

The use of the Malaxa tractor was widespread among the Romanian motorized units, so that during the invasion of the Soviet Union by the Axis forces, many units were lost destroyed or captured by the enemy; leaving only 50 Malaxa in service in the Romanian Army in 1943. The obsolescence of the Malaxa tractor forced the Romanian Army to withdraw them from active service in the front in 1943, to be used in mechanized training centers (as was the case with 33 Malaxa). The remaining 17 Malaxa were sent to the Malaxa facilities to be repaired, due to their bad shape.

Self-propelled Guns And Hybrid Tank Hunters
Of Romanian Manufacture

1) Vanatorul of Care R-35/45 (transformat)

As we have commented in the history of the R-35 tank within the Romanian Army, the 37mm main armament had been obsolete almost since the beginning of the war. To partially solve the problem, it was concluded the need for modernization. The modernization consisted of replacing its original gun with a 45 mm one, giving rise to the so-called Vanatorul de care R-35 (a tank hunter).

Since the conquest of Odessa and subsequent repairs to which the R-35 were submitted?, the possibility of replacing the R-35 turret with that of the Soviet T-26 (of which at least 33 units were captured for Romania) with a Soviet 45 mm 20K L/46 gun or even with a 47 mm Schneider gun.

The winner was the 20K L/46 gun because it was available in sufficient quantities when it came from both T-26 and BT-7 Soviet captured tanks.

The project was formally started on December 12, 1942 and was supervised by Colonel Constantin Ghiulai and Captain Dumitru Hogea.

The addition of the 45 mm gun in the turret showed a major problem, as there was no place to include a machine gun as secondary weapon. The first prototype was completed in February 1943, and the gun had a lifting motion of 25 degrees upwards and 8 degrees downwards.

The free space in the armored vehicle decreased due to the larger size of the 45 mm gun compared to the original 37 mm, as well as the larger size of the 45 mm projectiles; which motivated that only 35 projectiles could be transported.

For this modernization, 30 R-35s were chosen to be sent to the Leonida Company facilities. On the other hand, the guns with which they were going to equip the modernized R-35, were repaired in Târgoviste; to finally be assembled in the turret with its recoil system in the Concordia facilities near Ploieşti. In June of 1944 the 30 R-35/45 had been manufactured from the initials 30 R-35, being immediately sent to the 2nd Tank Regiment (from where the R-35s that had been sent for the modernization came). The new tank hunter improved the R-35 in firepower, although evidently it was not a first-class vehicle on the Eastern Front in 1944.

The continuity in the production was stopped due to the air bombing to which the Leonida facilities were subjected?; so the total number of R-35/45 produced, reached only 30 units. Also the Romania change of side stopped any type of work directed to produce new armored vehicles in Rumania. In this way, other projects based on the R-35 were also finalized.

The Vanatorul of care R-35 had a limited participation in the fighting, there being no record of its use against the Soviets but against the Germans and Hungarians (in fact there are several photographs where you can see the R-35/45 with the red star in its turret). In fact, they participated in the fighting in Austria and Czechoslovakia in the first months of 1945 until virtually no R-35/45 was left working?. The few R-35/45 that survived the war, shortly after the end of the war, were scrapped.

Comparative table between hybrid tank hunters of Romanian manufacture:

	Nationality	Crew	Weight (ton)	Main weapon (mm)	Speed Km/h	Main armor (mm)
R-35/45	Romania	2	11.7	45	20	40-44
TACAM T-60	Romania	3	9	76.2	40	35
TACAM R-2	Romania	3	12	76.2	30	17
MAREŞAL (M-05)	Romania	2	10	75	45	35

2) TACAM T-60

Another tank destroyer originated by the effort of the Romanian armaments industry to increase the anti-tank capacity of Romania. The then Lieutenant Colonel Constantin Ghiulai after his proposal of a tank destroyer was commissioned to design several of them from both own tanks and captured as chassis, and guns of Soviet origin as weapons.

In the case of the TACAM T-60, we are talking about a hybrid between the chassis of a tank T-60 (from the captured by the Romanians during the previous years of war) and a cannon also Soviet 76.2 mm M1939 F-22, reinforced by 15 mm armored plates for the protection of the crew from BT-7 tanks. At that time, Târgoviste had 38 copies of this 76.2 mm gun.

One of the reasons that determined that the T-60 was chosen as a chassis for the TACAM was that it had a GAZ 202 engine of 70-80 hp (which was a FH2 manufactured by the Soviets with license) of which there were abundant spare parts both in Germany and in Romania. The name of the new vehicle was, as we have said: TACAM T-60.

In addition to receiving the new gun, in the original T-60 chassis various modifications were made to the chassis and other components to get greater performance. The new vehicle was finally built for a three men crew: driver, commander-trigger and loader.

As early as January 12, 1943, a first prototype of the TACAM T-60 had already been manufactured, which was received with great acceptance due to its functional similarity to the German Marder (in which it was inspired) but with greater speed and a lower profile that would facilitate survival in the battlefield. The barrel had an elevation movement of 8 degrees upward, 5 degrees downward and 32 degrees lateral. To begin the conversion to the new vehicle, 23 T-60s were sent in working conditions to the Leonida industries in Bucharest (the total of T-60 sent to be transformed reached the 34 copies).

After the first prototype another 11 T-60s began to be transformed.

There were 17 copies of the TACAM T-60 that were sent at the end of June 1943 in a first batch to the 1st Tank Regiment of the 1st Armored Division and the Mechanized Training Center to be tested under conditions in real conditions. Subsequently, a second batch of another 17 TACAM T-60 that were completed at the end of 1943 were sent before the end of the year to the 1st Armored Division. The total of 34 TACAM T-60 was finally distributed 16 in the 1st Tank Regiment and 18 in the 2nd Tank Regiment; integrated into the 61st and 62nd TACAM Companies respectively.

Although in general little is known about? the use of the TACAM T-60 in the combat front, what it is known is that between February and August 1944 they participated in various confrontations with the Soviets in Bessarabia and Moldova.

After the Romania change of side, one of the demands of the Soviets was the delivery of all the arms captured by Romania to the Soviet Union; so the continuity of the TACAM T-60 ended up being built with chassis and Soviet guns. For this reason all the TACAM T-60s in service with the Romanian Army had to be returned to the USSR in October 1944.

3) TACAM R-2

This self-propelled gun was a hybrid between the R-2 and a 76 mm Soviet gun and was born as a project of the Romanian armament industry as a result of the disaster that meant the performance of the Romanian tanks against the Soviets in the Stalingrad Front. There were several projects that were made to improve the firepower of Romanian armored vehicles, such as the R-35/45 at the request of Colonel Constantin Ghiulai. In the spring of 1943 the Romanian Minister of War, General Constantin Pantazi, gave authorization for the work to begin on the conversion of a prototype from an R-2 that would eventually lead to the so-called Tun Anticar pe Afet Mobil R-2 or TACAM R-2 (the meaning of TACAM was self-propelled anti-tank gun). Again the name of Constantin Ghiulai was the one chosen to carry out this project that would be performed in Leonida's facilities in Bucharest between July and September of 1943. In this project it was thought that equipping the tank R-2 with an antitank piece of greater caliber was needed but faced with the impossibility of making compatible the new gun and the turret of the R-2, they had to decide the most suitable formula among several possibilities, like using the turret of a T-26 or the one from a BT-7, but no longer as a tank but as a tank destroyer or self-propelled gun.

The gun chosen initially in the prototype was the Soviet 76.2 mm M1936 F22 also coming from the spoils of war. The gun was installed in a superstructure with three closed sides (made with armored plates of captured BT-7 and T-26 tanks.) Thanks to this gun, Romanian armored vehicles would have real capacity to destroy the ubiquitous Soviet T-34 even at a distance between 500 and 600 meters using Romanian-made Constantinescu projectiles (the TACAM R-2 could carry 30 projectiles, 21 HE and 9 AP). Later it was thought that the Soviet 76.2 mm M1942 ZIS-3 gun could offer better performance, as well as the gun sights? which were replaced by others from national manufacture. Despite the evident improvement in fire capacity, the result was far from being the most adequate, since the T-34 could destroy the TACAM R-2 from a distance of at least 3000 meters, while? the new JS-2 tanks (which appeared on the Transnitria Front and Moldova) were practically invulnerable.

The first tests of the new prototype of TACAM took place in the Suditi training facilities, where the great improvement in firepower with respect to the original R-2 was appreciated, but it could also be verified that the general profile of the TACAM R-2 was too high so it made him an easy target. On the other hand, the driving of TACAM R-2 and R-2 were quite similar.

After the good impressions of the prototype of the TACAM R-2 compared to those of the original R-2, and before the imperative necessity of new armored vehicles the Romanian HQ understood the necessary conversion of all the R-2 available in the TACAM R-2, but it found the negative of General Mihail Racovita who refused to "release" the R-2 belonging to the 1st Armored Division until they were replaced by other tanks. All this did nothing but delaying the conversion of the R-2, so they had to wait until February 12, 1944 when the order was finally given from the War Ministry to convert 40 R-2 into the new TACAM R-2.

Finally the chosen gun was the mentioned 76.2 mm M1942 ZIS-3 for its better ballistic performance that was fitted on the chassis of the R-2. The gun had a lift movement of 15 degrees up, 5 degrees down and 30 degrees lateral. Between February and June 1944 the Leonida facilities began top transform a first batch of 20 R-2 that were previously withdrawn from those belonging to the 1st Tank Regiment.

It was not until the month of July 1944 that the first 7 TACAM R-2 were tested successfully in the training camp in Dadilov at the Mihai Bravu training center. In these tests prior to being delivered to the combat units, the TACAM R-2 showed a series of deficiencies in the aiming system, although there was not much time to solve this problem.

This fact, together with the imminent Soviet attack in Transnitria and Moldova, motivated the stop of the transformation of the second batch of 20 R-2 in the TACAM R-2 from the Motomechanized Troops High Command on July 22. In this way, the total production of this model was the 20 units of the first series together with the initial prototype.

In order to improve the performance of the TACAM R-2, it was thought to replace the Soviet guns with the Rumanian manufacture 75mm Reşiţa M1943 or the 88mm Krupp M1937. Another idea was to turn them into flamethrower tanks. But in the end all these improvements were never carried out due to the internal and external situation of Romania in mid-1944.

The 75mm Reşiţa gun was quite similar in performance to the German 75mm PaK 40, and therefore specially designed for anti-tank use. It could penetrate 100 mm of armor with an inclination of 30 degrees at a distance of about 500 meters. Several of these formidable guns were used in the last days of Rumania before changing of side, but in its towed version.

The use of TACAM R-2 in combat began when it was deployed in July into the 1st Tank Regiment (the R-2 that were transformed to the TACAM R-2 model came from here) within the 63rd Tank Destroyer Company. Not much is known of his performance against the Soviets during the August 1944 offensive. The use of the TACAM R-2 in the days after the Romanian change of side, compared to the Germans, is better known. In September of 1944 the number of TACAM R-2 in service had diminished to 6 units that were transferred to the 2nd Tank Regiment. They participated with this unit in various battles against Hungarian and Romanian troops in Austria and Czechoslovakia in the first months of 1945. On April 20, 1945 still 2 TACAM R-2 were still in service. The attrition of the 2nd Tank Regiment after the combats with little possibility of reparation, motivated that only one specimen survived at the end of the war. A single copy today is exhibited at the National Military Museum in Bucharest.

4) TACAM R-1

Another unfinished project to convert an armored vehicle into a tank destroyer or tank hunter was the one that tried to convert the surviving R-1 into TACAM R-1.

In this case the small size of the R-1 just allowed a 45 mm gun to be added, for which the Soviet M1942 was chosen.

The official proposal for this transformation took place on November 22, 1943, the subject was the 14 R-1 that were still in working condition.

The reason why this modernization project was not carried out was the nonsense of the great industrial effort to manufacture a TACAM with a 45 mm gun that was too heavy for the R-1 and that would have created important problems when it came to utilization.

5) TACAM T-38

Following the same guidelines that led to the birth of the TACAM R-2 or the TACAM T-60, also the T-38 resulted in a new TACAM Project, the so-called TACAM T-38.

Due to the characteristics of the T-38, the replacement of the original turret by a casemate with an anti-tank gun, should have resulted in an armored vehicle similar to the German Marder III. The main difference was that the cannon that the Romanians chose was the Soviet 76.2 mm F-22, of which at first Romania had 40 copies for this project.

Actually the TACAM T-38 remained as a project that never saw the light due to various causes, although the main one was the paralysis of any development of the Romanian arms industry after the change of side of Romania followed by the immediate and mandatory delivery of all the Soviet material that the Romanians had captured during the previous years of war.

6) MAREŞAL

The great inferiority in terms of Romanian armored power with respect to that of its Soviet rivals led, as we have commented previously, to numerous programs aimed at improving it. Perhaps the project that could have been the most decisive for Romania was that of the Mareşal tank hunter.

The limitations of the Romanian armament industry did not allow the manufacture of medium or heavy tanks, devoting its greatest effort to improving the performance of various armored vehicles present in the Romanian arsenal, basically adding larger caliber guns. But in the case of the Mareşal (which means Marshal in Romanian), it was an attempt to create a new armored vehicle of very high benefits with an adequate armor and a powerful armament; although at first also starting from captured Soviet material.

It was in December 1942 when Marshal Antonescu (after who Mareşal name is) ordered the manufacture of a self-propelled gun or light tank destroyer. In the experts team chosen for the design of the Mareşal were Major Nicolae Anghel, Captain Gheorghe Sambotin, Colonel Ghiulai and others , who had to create an armored vehicle from material originated in the national industry or of Soviet origin.

The project of the Mareşal was changing as its design was progressing. The first prototype, called project M-00 Mareşal, consisted of a chassis of a Soviet tank T-60 to which the turret and the original armor was removed to replace them with a new angled shield of 20-30 mm that gave it a certain resemblance with the shell of a turtle. The crew consisted of two persons and the armament consisted of the Soviet 122 mm M1910/1930 Soviet Putulv-Obuhov howitzer and a coaxial 7.92 mm ZB-53 machine gun. The vehicle had a Ford V8 85-hp engine built under license, which was sufficient for proper management of the Mareşal. This first prototype was completed during the first months of 1943 and was subjected to various trials on July 30, 1943. For the howitzer they were working simultaneously in the manufacture of HEAT HL (Hochladung) projectiles for anti-tank use.

The result of the trials in the first Mareşal prototype can be considered to be quite positive, but far from perfect. Apart from the good handling behavior and adequate stability, several problems were seen in terms of engine power and recoil movement of the main weapon, among others.

From the knowledge acquired in the first prototype, Marshal Antonescu asked the Rogifer industry to build three more prototypes. These three new prototypes called M-01, M-02 and M-03 were built between July and October 1943 with various modifications with respect to the M-00 while maintaining its armor (and therefore its profile so characteristic) and armament.

A significant variation was the improvement of the engine, going from the 85 hp of the original engine to the 120 hp of the new Buick engine. Work was also done to improve the suspension system of the vehicle, which was reinforced, leading to a significant improvement in this aspect. Only the M-03 showed certain differences with its "brothers", since it presented a more elongated chassis, reinforced internal structure, welded armor, better assembly of the main weapon and a reduction in the thickness of the armor (10 mm).

The configuration of the Mareşal crew was as follows: driver and gun pointer on the right side, and the loader beside him.

On October 23, 1943 the three new prototypes were subjected to various tests in the Suditi training field. Again the results were very promising, but new and old problems (already appreciated in the M-00) were detected. The 122mm howitzer, due to its weight, was the cause of a significant reduction in vehicle performance. On the other hand, the power of the engine was more adequate than that of the M-00, but the Buick engine was not available in sufficient quantities, so it was unviable to use it in a mass production.

Before these two main problems, feasible solutions were sought in Romania at the end of 1943 for a new Mareşal prototype. On one hand, it was decided to re-place the Buick engine with the Hotchkiss, also with 120 hp and manufactured in France (1,000 copies were requested in November 1943); on the other, it was also decided to replace the Soviet howitzer with a new 75 mm M1943 Reşiţa anti-tank gun (DT-UDR 26) of Romanian manufacture (based on the German Pak 40). On the same day that the three prototypes were tested, the Reşiţa gun was also tested, so Antonescu was pleasantly surprised; and at the request of Colonel Paul Draghiescu (who was part of the Mareşal design team) he approved the change of the Soviet howitzer to the Romanian gun.

The basis of the design of the Mareşal is very similar to those that gave rise to various German tank destroyers. In fact, there were contacts between Romanian and German manufacturers in this regard, concluding that the Romanian model had even better performance than the Germans. It is no coincidence that the manufacturing order of the German Jagdpanzer 38t "Hetzer" tank destroyer was in December 1943. Although the Hetzer and Mareşal were not the same, they did share many charac-teristics in terms of design and low profile. Unfortunately for Romania, the produc-tion of the Mareşal can not be compared at all with the production of the Hetzer.

The Romanian expert committee, after assessing the M-01, M-02 and M-03, finally opted for the M-03 with engine and gun modifications to start mass production.

The new prototype of Mareşal, the M-04 incorporated all the improvements mentioned above, was built as quickly as possible and was tested in February 1944 in Suditi with the presence of OKH German officers. Again the results were very encouraging, since the various improvements of the project (from the prototype M-00) had had its effect. But again some doubts were raised again about the chas-sis and hull of the T-60 that had the Mareşal, which continued making problems in terms of the suspension of the vehicle. As we said earlier, the Germans were developing the Hetzer, which was based on the chassis of a Pz.38; so in March 1944 the Romanian engineers thought that due to the better suspension of Pz.38, this tank of Czechoslovak origin could be the right chassis on which to create the new Mareşal prototype.

Immediately proceeded to the construction of two new prototypes, the M-05 and the M-06, both on the chassis of the Pz. 38. The engine was the French Hotchkiss, the gearbox was French, the gun was the 75 mm Reşiţa, the suspensions and tracks were Czechoslovak and the radio and optics were of German origin. Having to get the different parts in such diverse origins was a great effort for Romania, although by then and due to the great German interest in the Mareşal, some specialists from the German industries Alkett and Vomag began to collaborate on the project. With respect to the Reşiţa gun, it is important to mention that 1100 units were ordered in December 1943, although in February 1944 there were only 30 units in service.

In May of 1944 the first of the two new prototypes was finished, so in July it was presented to Marshal Antonescu and he proceeded to submit it to various tests. After the evaluation of the results, it was concluded that most of the problems that the previous prototypes had, were solved.

The Romanian High Command was delighted with the Mareşal, so it was thought to produce 1000 units to form 32 anti-tank battalions with them. In fact, to facilitate the integration of the Mareşal into the armored units, a training battalion called M Battalion was formed within the 2nd Tank Regiment.

It was estimated that the monthly production of the Mareşal should be 100 units per month as of September 1944, a fact that could never be completed due to the evolution of the fighting in the Romanian Front.

At last Romania had managed to build a modern national armor (albeit with multinational components) with great performance that was at the same level or even above the German tank destroyers of the year 1944. The next step was the start of mass production for what a cooperation agreement was signed with Germany on June 8, 1944 to supply Romania with 10 chassis of Pz.38 and the manufacturing license of the engine AC Prague 160 hp. The latter was motivated by the destruction of the industrial facilities of Hotchkiss in France by Allied bombing. At that time, the Mareşal was a weapon awaited in the Axis, not only by Romania but also by Germany, which also had the intention of acquiring enough copies of the Romanian tank destroyer. In fact, in June, a fire and mobility comparison test was conducted between a StuG III and a Mareşal, with the Romanian vehicle being the winner.

As we can see, Romania tried to move the Mareşal forward, but to the difficulty of obtaining the components of such varied origins we had to add the Allied bombings on the Romanian industries and what was even worse: the next Soviet offensive on Romania, which took place in August of 1944.

The tests on the M-05 continued on July 24 and August 21 trying to improve the project. Despite the complicated situation, when the project was canceled in 1944 due to the Romania change of side, it was going to start imminently the building of the first 10 Mareşal, and it was even planned a variant built with a 220 hp Tatra T-engine 103.

After the arrival of the Soviets, on October 26 all plans of the Mareşal as well as the prototype M-05 were confiscated, thus ending the promising history of the best Romanian tank destroyer.

From this promising vehicle, a new project was developed that turned the Mareşal into an anti-aircraft vehicle called Flakpanzer Mareşal equipped with two 37 mm anti-aircraft fast guns. In this case, unlike the Mareşal, it never left the design paper.

Armored Vehicles Of German Origin

1) TA-3 or TA T-3

The arrival of the TA-3 to Romania (name given by the Romanians to the StuG IIIG) occurred after the practical destruction of the 1st Armored Division in the fighting for Stalingrad. Recall that the TA-3s were included within the Olivenbaum Program (on September 23, 1943 the Germans agreed to carry out the armored delivery program called Olivenbaum I, which should be followed for the II and III), proceeded to the sale of German armored material between the months of November 1943 and July 1944 in exchange for Romanian fuel fundamentally. This motivated that 108 TAs (StuG IIIG) were delivered between November 1943 and August 1944. The name TA comes from the Romanian Tun of Asalt or assault cannon. The G model of the Stug III, which was received by the Romanians, represented the definitive evolution of the Stug III as tank destroyers (tank hunters). In addition it had an improved shield of 80 mm in the frontal zone and lateral skirts for the protection against antitank weapons.

These self-propelled guns had already proved their worth in the German Army with their powerful 75 mm gun capable of destroying most of the enemy tanks without any problems, for which they represented a significant increase in the fighting capacity of the Romanian armored units. Specifically the TAs were deployed in the 1st Armored Division, the 8th Motorized Cavalry Division, the 4th Army Armored Detachment and in smaller numbers in the Tárgovişte Mechanized Training Center.

The text discusses Romania's use of TAs in more detail. Like with the T-4, many of the armored property owned by Romania were used or seized by the Germans in the Soviet offensive in August 1944. After the Romanian change of side some of the surviving TA were requisitioned by the Soviets, passing others to form part of the 2nd Tank Regiment in their combats in Czechoslovakia and Austria. The TA of the 2nd Tank Regiment at the end of the war were all out of service.

	Nationality	Crew	Weight (ton)	Main weapon (mm)	Speed Km/h	Main armor (mm)
StuG III G (TA)	Germany	4	23.9	75 mm	40	80
Pz IIIM (T-3)	Germany	5	21.1	75 mm	40	80
Pz IV F1 (T-4)	Germany	5	22.3	75 mm	42	80
Pz IV F2 (T-4)	Germany	5	23.6	75 mm	40	80
Pz IV H (T-4)	Germany	5	26	75 mm	38	80
Pz 38 (T-38)	Czechoslovakia (Germany)	4	10.5	37 mm	42	50

2) T-3

The alarmingly low performance that the Romanian tanks had demonstrated during Operation Barbarossa and in Odessa, showed the real Romanian armored power. In view of the need to obtain modern tanks, as mentioned in the text, modern armored material was requested from Germany. Among the armored vehicles that Romania received was the Panzerkampfwagen III.

On October 17, 1942 Germany agreed to deliver 11 Panzerkampfwagen III Ausf N equipped with a short 75 mm KwK L/24 low-speed gun (a good improvement within the Romanian arsenal, although still obsolete against its Soviet rivals) and two 7.92mm MG34machine guns. In Romania the denomination of the tank was T-3.

Immediately 10 T-3s were incorporated into the 1st Romanian Armored Division 1st Tank Regiment that was deployed in the Don river front, and 1 copy was sent to Romania for the crew training in the new armored vehicles (being assigned to the 2nd Tank Regiment).

These tanks, although in small numbers, provided an improvement in both the defensive and offensive capacity of the Romanian armored unit, but they came to the front line so close to the Soviet offensive (due to the battle for Stalingrad and Operation Uranus), that their crews only had three days to train before being involved in the ensuing combat. As already related in its corresponding chapter in this text, the 1st Tank Regiment was practically annihilated, which evidently happened to almost all the T-3 that participated in the clashes. After the repatriation of the 1st Tank Regiment, the 2 T-3s that were still in service in the Romanian Army were not used again until February of 1944 when they were included in the "Cantemir" Mixed Armored Group. Finally during the Soviet offensive of August 1944, the two T-3s were destroyed in the fight for the defense of Transnitria.

3) T4

The arrival of the Panzerkampfwagen IV G at Romania is based on the same fact that motivated the arrival of the Panzerkampfwagen III N in 1942, so we are not going to repeat the story. What can be said with certainty is that it was the first tank of the Romanian arsenal that could really face on equal combat capability a great part of its rivals from its arrival in 1942 until the end of the armed conflict. Unlike the 75mm KwK L/48 gun from the T-3, this tank has a long barrel and greater projectile exit velocity, which gave it greater destructive power against other armored vehicles. It also had two 7.92mm MG34 machine guns.

This tank in Romania was called T-4 and 11 were received (along with the 11 T-3) a few days before the beginning of the Soviet Stalingrad offensive in November 1942. They were considered heavy tanks (although in reality they were medium tanks) and 10 of them were destined to the 1st Romanian Armored Division 1st Tank Regiment and 1 T-4 was sent to Romania for crew training in the new armored vehicles (being assigned to the 2nd Tank Regiment). After the Romanian debacle and, of course, of the 1st Armored Division, it seems unlikely that any of the 10 T-4 would be saved, although some unreliable sources report that 2 or 3 were withdrawn to Romania in January-February 1943.

Germany was not unaware of Romania's peremptory need to get new modern tanks to have some fighting power after the practical destruction of the 1st Armored Division in the fighting for Stalingrad. Thanks to this, at the request of the Romanian Ministry of War Production Army and framed within the Olivenbaum Program (on September 23, 1943 the Germans agreed to carry out the armored delivery program called Olivenbaum I, which should follow by the II and III), proceeded to the sale of armored vehicles between the months of November 1943 and July 1944 in exchange for Romanian fuel fundamentally. The total number of T-4 received thanks to this Program amounted to 114 tanks PzKpfw IV (most of the tanks were Pz-IVH, but there were some F-2 and J). In fact 150 copies had been ordered, but by mid-August 1944 only 114 had been received, and the subsequent Romanian change of side prevented the arrival of more PzKpfw IV. Really it is very complicated to know with certainty the exact number according to the consulted source, thus for example according to Axworthy the number could reach up to 129.

The T-4s were deployed in various Romanian armored units such as the "Cantemir" Mixed Armored Group (30 T-4 in February 1944), the Fast Armored Detachment (32 units in March 1944) or the "Romania Mare's" 1st Tank Regiment (48 T-4 in August 1944). After the Rumanian change of side, the T-4 faced their old German and Hungarian allies, in diverse small armored units like the "Lt. Col. Gheorghe Matei" Armored Detachment or the 2nd Tank Regiment together with their new Soviet allies.

At the end of the war, the Romanians only had 1 operative T-4 (2 according to other sources).

4) T-38

This Czechoslovakian origin tank had its glory moment during the first two years of war, but when they arrived at Romanian hands in March 1943(they did not reach the battle front until three months later), they were already obsolete, poorly armed and scarcely armored, so they were weak adversaries of the Soviet armor.

As it was previously told in the text, after the Stalingrad debacle and the loss of most of the Romanian armored equipment, it was necessary to ask the German ally for new and modern tanks to rebuild the 1st Armored Division. But the German answer could not be more disappointing since the only material that was sent to them, as stipulated in the Birnbaum Program, were 50 Pzkpfw.38(t) that were not destined to Romania to be the core of the Division armored but, by German demand, had to be sent to the frontline combat in Crimea.

The Pzkpfw.38(t) was named in Romania as T-38 and was an improvement over the R-2 or R-35 although still inferior to its Soviet armored rivals and even to the anti-tank rifles. But a new problem shook the Romanians when receiving the new tanks they saw how many of them could not be used operationally; actually, of the 50 only 17 were ready for action. The reason was that they were tanks already used by the Germans during the war and that they were very worn. In addition the tanks had not received an adequate service before being delivered to their new owners.

Finally, thanks to the efforts of the Romanian mechanics and crews, they managed to put them all into operation.

In June 1943 they joined the so-called Batalionul care da lupta T-38 that was divided into three Companies: 51st Company, 52nd Company and 53rd Company, with 15 T-38 each; being attached to the Cavalry Corps. The remaining 5 T-38 remained in reserve although according to some source they acted as command unit (or 54th Company).

Although the combat zone where the T-38 fought was not a zone of great utilization of the tanks, due to its vulnerability to Soviet antitank weapons, several T-38s were destroyed or damaged.

Again the tactics of the Romanian armor were carried out, the tanks being the "protectors" of the infantry which they supported in their movements. The T-38s were never used together in order to break the enemy lines with a big armored blow.

Once back in Romania, in 1944, the use of the surviving T-38 was limited to certain actions against their former German ally in the "Victor Popescu", Armored Detachment possibly in Bucharest and Ploiești, or within the 2nd Tank Regiment in Austria and Czechoslovakia.

On April 22, 1945 the last 5 T-38s in service were seized by the Soviets, thus ending their participation in the war.

5) AB

The debacle of the Romanian armored troops after Stalingrad motivated the need to acquire new armored vehicles to put up the 1st Armored Division back into combat conditions. As we have seen during the pages of this text, the main Romanian objectives were the tanks, without forgetting the small reconnaissance armored vehicles so necessary in any armored unit. In fact, there were 10 AB (which was the name given to the SdKfz 222 armored reconnaissance vehicles of German manufacturing) in the operative force available to the Division just before the beginning of the operations aimed at the capture of Stalingrad. They formed the 1st Armored Division Reconnaissance Group and they were also located during the reform period of the 1st Armored Division.

Subsequently and in accordance with the Olivenbaum Program, 40 AB were supplied between November 1943 and August 1944. With them, the reconnaissance capacity of various Romanian units, especially the "Romania Mare", was enhanced. When the Soviet offensive took place in August 1944, "Romania Mare" had 12 armored reconnaissance vehicles (possibly with several ABs).

After the Romanian change of side, there is evidence of the existence of 5 AB in the "General Nicolescu" Armored Detachment Reconnaissance Group who participated in the actions for the capture of Transylvania in September 1944.

Subsequently, it is also known the existence of 8 AB in the 2nd Tank Regiment during his actions together with the Soviet Army.

6) TB

We must highlight the SdKfz 250 (SPW 250) and SdKfz 251 (SPW 251) or TB in Romania, among the Romanian armored vehicles. These armored half-track vehicles were integrated into the 1st Armored Division after being supplied to Romania between 1943 and 1944 within the Olivenbaum Plan. Its use varied from the transport of troops to the support of the infantry or for light attacks. Although they were not received in large numbers and had already been used before by the Germans, they did represent a significant improvement within the Romanian armored forces.

After the change of side of Rumania, it is known that at least 5 of these armored vehicles half-track were in service in the 2nd Regiment of tanks in March of 1945. Of them, 2 caused loss? during the combats and 3 survived the war.

7) FAMO

Although it is not exactly an armored vehicle, we include in this section this German origin half-track that was one of the most important artillery tractors available in the Romanian Army. Although it was manufactured in Germany from years before, several units of this vehicle arrived in Romania in 1943. As it was reasonable, these powerful vehicles went to some of the most important units of the Romanian Army: the 1st Romanian Armored Division and the 8th Division of Cavalry (which we remember was intended to convert into an armored unit as well).

These powerful vehicles with 250 hp could transport a weight of 2.8 tons or tow up to 8 tons and reach up to 50 km/h.

8) AUTOBLINDA 41

This small armored vehicle of Italian origin is included in this section since in September 1943, within the contingent of armored vehicles that the Germans sent to Romania thanks to the Olivenbaum Plan, there were 8 AB 41 (Autoblinda 41). These vehicles were captured by Germany to Italy after the change of side of Italy. Specifically, these 8 vehicles may have belonged to the Italian Expeditionary Corps in the Soviet Union.

These vehicles had a 20 mm cannon and reached a maximum speed of 78 km/h, which made them very suitable for reconnaissance tasks on the battle front.

Vehicles Captured By Romania

One of the ways to increase the Romanian armored arsenal consisted of the incorporation of the different tanks and other armored vehicles that were captured during the combats in which they took part. In some cases the shortage of spare parts for them, meant that they could not be used properly by their new owners.

Before the beginning of the World War II, the various movements of Germany over Poland and Czechoslovakia caused that in many situations, troops from these attacked countries sought refuge in neighboring countries. In this situation, the country that received the fugitives, immediately requisitioned any type of weapon they carried, so they were incorporated into the Romanian arsenal. We remember the 34 R-35 from the 21st Polish Light Tank Battalion that were requisitioned by Romania, although they will not be commented here since they were in their corresponding section.

During the years in which Romania took part in the World War II, many armored vehicles were captured by the Soviets and put in service with the Romanian armored forces. In March 1944 a large number of captured armored vehicles were transported to Romania, including 41 tanks (according to Axworthy they were 4 T-34s, 4 T-38s, 4 Lees, 4 Valentine Mk IIIs, 1 KVIs, 5 Stuarts and 19 others unspecified).

Towards the end of 1942 it is estimated that about 175 armored vehicles and 154 artillery guns of different caliber had been captured. We have already commented how some of them were used for the construction of new vehicles, such as the

TACAM T-60 or the first Mareşal prototype. Others were used directly without being subjected to any transformation due to the urgent need to have more armored vehicles.

Later after the change of side of Rumania, the armored vehicles captured were Germans and Hungarians. In this case the severe Soviet control over Romanian armored vehicles did not allow them to dispose of the captured vehicles for a long time. Between the months of February and May of 1945, the 2nd Tank Regiment also received several armored vehicles captured from the Germans by the Soviets, mainly Pz.IVs and StuGs.

The main vehicles seized or captured were:

1) OA vz 27

Three units of this armored vehicle were requisitioned to a Czechoslovak squad that took refuge in Romania in March 1939. These vehicles were not used in combat, but in internal security and surveillance missions; 2 of them were destroyed during the American bombings in Ploieşti over 1944.

2) OA vz.30

Like its "brother" vehicle OA vz 27, they arrived at the Romanian arsenal after the flight of a Czech company in March 1939 that ended up seeking refuge in Romania. In this case 9 copies were seized, of which its subsequent use is unknown. It is very possible that, like the OA vz.27, they were used in surveillance tasks and not in combat. In fact, some report places them in the Antonescu´s escort unit (Batalionul de gardă al Mareşal ului Antonescu or Regimentul de gardă al Conducătorului Statului). Three units were destroyed in the American bombings over Ploieşti.

3) FORD RUSESC DE CAPTURA

As we have seen throughout the text, Romania captured various types of armor during its campaign in the Soviet Union. One of the least known was the Komsomolets artillery tractor. It was a vehicle designed in 1936 from the chassis of the Soviet armored T-38, of which 7780 units were built that reached speeds of 47.5 km/h. It was a vehicle that was used as an artillery tractor as well as a light tank or ammunition transport and that was armed with a DT 7.62 mm machine gun (it had two crew and had capacity for 6 more people). As the main negative aspect, we must bear in mind that the thickness of its armor was so small that it made it vulnerable to infantry weapons fire.

Romania managed to capture several dozens of this artillery tractor in various operative status during the years 1941 and 1942. Due to the general poor condition of the Komsomolets (in many cases the engines had been damaged by their owners before being abandoned), they had to be sent to Romania where they were subjected to various maintenance and repair work to put them into operative status. The Romanian engineers had luck in their favor, since the original engine of the artillery tractor was a Ford built under license, and in Romania, in the factory Rogifer (in Bucharest), was the Ford-Romanian Truck Factory (fabrica de autocamioane Ford-Romana) that was able to put in working condition up to 34 Komsomolets using spare parts between April and October 1943. After that, between January and March 1944 they received several modifications among which it is necessary to emphasize that some hooks were added in the industries Parvan Marian that allowed them to pull the 50 mm PaK 38 anti-tank guns. Although the 50 mm gun at the time was completely outdated and inadequate to deal with Soviet tanks, for the Romanian Army it represented an increase in its mobile anti-tank capability.

After the modifications made to Soviet vehicles, the Komsomolets received a new name in Romania, the Ford rusesc de captura.

They were immediately sent to the front of Moldova, distributed by various units (at least the 5th and 14th Infantry Divisions received 12 each, the 2nd Tank Regiment received 2 and the 5th Cavalry Division received 4) where some were destroyed during the Soviet offensive in August 1944, although most were captured by the attackers.

4) T-26

It is known that at least 33 units of this obsolete light tank were captured by the Romanians during their campaign in the Soviet Union. According to sources, it seems that they did have some use in combat at the hands of the Romanians against their previous owners.

5) T-60

The T-60 was so useless in its use in combat that the Romanians never tried to put it into service in its original configuration. Most of the T-60s captured were used as the basis for the construction of the TACAM T-60.

6) T-34

There were few T-34 captured by the Romanians, but their great value resulted in some T-34 being placed in service against their previous owners. The lack of spare parts was the main problem of these tanks in Romanian hands, which caused them to be out of service in a short time (according to some sourcess 2 units were used in November 1942). Other captured T-34s (possibly at least 4) were sent to Romania to study them and serve as an object of the training of Romanian anti-tank troops.

Although Antonescu was interested in the possibility of copying the T-34, the real capabilities of the Romanian industry could never carry out this desire.

After the change of side, all tanks of Soviet origin were immediately requisitioned.

7) BA-10 and BA-64

During the first years of Romania's participation in the Eastern Front, several operative BA-10 and BA-64 were captured. It is unknown the subsequent use that the Romanians made of these DT 7.62 mm machine gun armed armored cars.

8) SEVERAL CAPTURED ARMORED VEHICLES

During the years of war against the Soviet Union and the months in fight against Germany, other armored vehicles were captured, of which little is known. Possibly some were used temporarily (until the shortage of spare parts forced to give up its use) or some could never even be put at the service of the Romanian Army. According to some source, in 1943 some American origin M3A tanks were captured, in 1944 1 JS-2 and 1 ISU-152 were captured; and after the change of side of Rumania in 1944 at least 2 Pz.II.

Possibly more armored vehicles were captured in small numbers, but there is practically no information about them, this being the reason for grouping them in this chapter.

9) HETZER

Two of this magnificent tank hunter armed with a 75 mm L/48 gun were captured between September and October 1944 in operative conditions by Romanian troops during the fighting against Hungarians and Germans in Transylvania.

They were incorporated to the Romanian armored forces with which they intervened in successive combats until the Soviets had information of it, after which they were immediately requisitioned.

10) ZRÍNYI II

A single copy of this Hungarian-made self-propelled gun was captured by the Romanians in Transylvania during the months of September and October 1944. The Zrínyi II (40/43M Zrinyi II) reached 43 km/h on road and carried a 105 mm howitzer (40/43M L/20.5). As with the two captured Hetzer units, the Zrínyi II was used in combat until the Soviets seized it following the guidelines received from Moscow.

Never Born Projects

There were several armored vehicles that Romania tried to put into service within its Army but were never built. Some of this projects were not accomplished because of the politics in the tumultuous Europe of the beginning of the 40s, while others were attempts by the Romanian industry to improve the national arsenal, also being definitively postponed due to the evolution of the armed conflict.

Some of these vehicles are:

1) R-3

This is the tank of Czechoslovak origin that was in the production line after the LT vz. 35 and it was called T-21. It was a 17-ton tank and armed with a 47 mm gun, which in one of its variants (T-22) became the 40M Turán I Hungarian tank. The Romanian interest in this tank began when in 1940 the supply of tanks R-35 was slowed by the conquest of France by Germany. Quickly alternatives were sought and this tank was shown as a solution to the problem.

The number of tanks that Romania wanted to acquire was 216 (287 according to other sources) being called R-3, but the intervention of Germany together with the limited Romanian industrial capacity prevented any type of acquisition of this tank.

2) T-1

The T-1 was a tractor vehicle developed by the Romanian industry, in particular by Ford in Bucharest, which should have been manufactured in series during the years 1944 and 1945 to equip the Romanian Army with an adequate vehicle to pull the Romanian Reşiţa gun. It was based on the Soviet STZ tractor that after being studied was considered very suitable to be used in the Romanian Army. Five T-1 were manufactured until 1944 but its production was suspended because the Romanian industry did not have T-1 as a priority.

3) REMOTE CONTROL VEHICLE

This little known Romanian design of remote control vehicle had similar characteristics to the German Goliath, which caused it to be called the Romanian Goliath. There is no record about if this vehicle was beyond the design paper in 1944. The capabilities of this 2 ton weight prototype should have been similar to the Goliath.

Annex 3: Romanian Army Ranks

In this annex we show the Romanian Army ranks compared to their homonyms in German Army and in Americans and British. Based in Axworthy and Mollo works.

Romanian	German	English
Maresal al România	Generalfeldmarschall	General of the Army/Field Marshal
General de armatâ	Generaloberst	General
General de corp de armatâ	General der Infanterie	Lieutenant General
General de divizie	Generalleutnant	Major General
General de brigadâ	Generalmajor	Brigadier General/Brigadier
Colonel	Oberst	Colonel
Locotenent-colonel	Oberstleutnant	Lieutenant Colonel
Maior	Major	Major
Căpitan	Hauptmann	Captain
Locotenent	Oberleutnant	Lieutenant
Sublocotenent	Leutnant	2nd Lieutenant
Plutonier adjutant	-	-
Plutonier major	-	-
Plutonier	-	-
Sergent major	Oberfeldwebel	Master Sergeant/Warrant Officer Class I
Sergent	Unterfeldwebel	Staff Sergeant/Sergeant
Caporal	Unteroffizier	Sergeant/Corpora
Fruntas	Gefreiter	Lance Corporal
Soldat	Schütze	Private

Bibliography

Antill, Peter. El sitio de Stalingrado. Osprey Publishing. 2001.

Axworthy, Mark. Third Axis Fourth Ally. Arms and Armour. 1995.

Axworthy, Mark. The Romanian Army of Worls War II. Osprey Publishing. 2005.

Beavor, Antony. Stalingrado. Memoria Crítica. 2002.

Becze, Csaba. Magyar Steel. Stratus. 2006.

Bernád, Denes; Kliment, Charles K. Magyar warriors. The history of the Royal Hungarian Armed Forces 1919-1945. Volume I. Helion & Company. 2015.

Bernád, Denes; Kliment, Charles K. Magyar warriors. The history of the Royal Hungarian Armed Forces 1919-1945. Volume II. Helion & Company. 2017.

Bernád, Denes. Rumanian Air Force. The prime decade 1938-1947. Squadron/signal Publications.1999.

Caballero, C; Molina, L. Panzer IV. El puño de la Wehrmacht. AF Editores. 2006.

Cloutier, P.Three Kings: Axis Royal Armies on the Russian Front 1941. 2015.

Cloutier, P.Three Kings: Axis Royal Armies on the Russian Front 1942. 2015.

Consulado de Rumania en Sevilla (Romanian Consulate in Seville).

Di Giusto, Stefano. Panzer-Sicherungs-Kompanieb and Panzer-Abteilung 208-I./Panzer-Regiment Feldherrnhalle. Tankograd Publishing. 2010.

Filipescu, Mihai T. Reluctant Axis : The Romanian Army in Russia. 1941-1944. FTM.

Gil Martínez, Eduardo Manuel. Fuerzas acorazadas húngaras 1939-45. Almena. 2017.

Gladysiak, L; Karmieh, S. Panzer IV Ausf. H and Ausf.J. Vol I. Kagero 2015.

Gladysiak, L; Karmieh, S. Panzer IV Ausf. H and Ausf.J. Vol II. Kagero 2016.

Glantz, David M., House, Jonathan M.Choque de titanes. La victoria del Ejército Rojo sobre Hitler. Ediciones Desperta Ferro. 2017.

Heiber, Hemut. Hitler y sus generales. Memoria Crítica. 2005.

Höpper, Wolf. Against the Flood. The Russian Juggernaut Strikes Successfully for the First Time. GALEFORCE NINE

https://www.militar.org.ua/foro/la-operacion-urano-y-el-puente-aereo-de-stalingrado-t33374.html

https://forum.axishistory.com//viewtopic.php?t=73749

http://ftr.wot-news.com/2014/05/14/romanian-tanks-addendum/

https://www.facebook.com/RomanianArmyWorldWar2/

https://forum.axishistory.com/viewtopic.php?f=4&t=8113&start=30

http://www.historynet.com/romanian-nightmare-stalingrad.htm

http://www.tanks-encyclopedia.com/ww2/romanian-tanks-ww2.php

http://gmic.co.uk/

https://thearmoredpatrol.com/2016/03/20/romanian-tank-destroyers-in-world-of-tanks/

http://codenames.info/operation/trajan-linie/

Instituto Cultural Rumano en España (Romanian Cultural Institute in Spain).

Jacobsen, Hans-Adolf, Dollinger, Hans. La Segunda Guerra Mundial. La ofensiva Aliada se impone. Tomo 7. Plaza & Janes. 1989.

Joly, Anton. Stalingrad Battle Atlas. Volume III. Stal. 2015-2017.

Lentz, Thomas L. Panzer Truppen. Vol 2. Schiffer Military History. 1996.

Miller, David. Tanks of the world. Greenwich Editions.2001.

Mollo, Andrew. The armed forces of World War II. Uniforms, Insignia & organization. Greenwich Editions. 2000.

Mujzer, Peter. Hungarian Armored Forces in Worls War II. Kagero. 2017.

Mujzer, Peter. Huns on wheels. Mujzer&Partner Ltd.

Muñoz, Roberto. Bagration y las ofensivas soviéticas de 1944. Almena. 2010.

Nafziger, George F. Rumanian Order of Battle in World War II.

Scafes, Cornel; Scafes, Ioan I; Serbanescu, Horia VL. Trupele Blindata dun Armata Romana 1919-1947. Oscar Print. 2005.

Several authors. Frente del Este. Vehículos rusos 1935-1945. Ammo of Mig Jiménez. 2014.

Spaeter, Helmuth. The history of Panzerkorps Grossdeutschland. Vol 2. J.J. Fedorowicz Publishing. 1995.

Thomas, Nigel; Pál Szábo, László. The Royal Hungarian Army in World War II. Osprey Publishing. 2008.

Tirone, Laurent. Panzer. The German tanks encyclopedia. Caraktere. 2016.

Turner, Wayne; Yates, Phil. Romanian Cavalry Division Mid-war Batalion de Cavalerie. Flames of war.2015.

Turner, Wayne. The Romanian Army in World War II. Web Flames of war.

Villamor, Rubén. La batalla del Kubán 1943. Almena. 2017.

Web Axisafvs.blogspot

Web Historice.ro

Web russkiivopros.com

Web Worldwar2.ro

Web World War Photos

Wikipedia. Several articles.

Zaloga, Steven J. El Ejército Rojo en la Gran Guerra Patriótica. Osprey Publishing. 2010.

Zaloga, Steven J. Soviet lend-lease tanks of World War II. Osprey Publishing. 2017.

Zaloga, Steven J. Tanks of Hitler´s eastern allies. 1941-45. Osprey Publishing. 2013.

Ziemke, Earl F. Stalingrad to Berlin: The German Defeat in the East. Center of Military History United States Army Washington, D. C., 1987